AI for Theological Education

AI for Theological Education

under the supervision of
Thomas E. Phillips

Theological Essentials

©Digital Theological Library 2025
Library of Congress Cataloging-in-Publication Data

Thomas E. Phillips (creator).
    AI for Theological Education / Thomas E. Phillips
120 + xiii pp. cm. 12.7 x 20.32
ISBN 979-8-89731-588-8 (Print)
ISBN 979-8-89731-132-3 (Ebook)
ISBN 979-8-89731-134-7 (Kindle)
ISBN 979-8-89731-144-6 (Abridged Audio Discussion)
  1. Theological education — Technological innovations
  2. Religious education — Technological innovations
  3. Seminaries — Curricula — Technological innovations
BV4019 .P55 2025

This book is available in other languages at
www.DTLPress.com

Cover Image: AI-generated revision of Michelangelo's painting of
God reaching out to Adam.
Photo credit: DTL Staff, using AI

Contents

Series Preface

Artificial Intelligence (AI) is changing everything, including theological scholarship and education. This series, *Theological Essentials*, is designed to bring the creative potential of AI to the field of theological education. In the traditional model, a scholar with both mastery of the scholarly discourse and a record of successful classroom teaching would spend several months—or even several years—writing, revising and rewriting an introductory text which would then be transferred to a publisher who also invested months or years in production processes. Even though the end product was typically quite predictable, this slow and expensive process caused the prices of textbooks to balloon. As a result, students in developed nations paid more than they should have for the books and students in developing nations typically had no access to these (cost-prohibitive) textbooks until they appeared as discards and donations decades later. In previous generations, the need for quality assurance—in the form of content generation, expert review, copy-editing and printing time—may have made this slow, expensive and exclusionary approach inevitable. However, AI is changing everything.

This series is very different; it is created by AI. The cover of each volume identifies the work as "created under the supervision of" an expert in the field. However, that person is not an author in the traditional sense. The creator of each volume has been trained by the DTL staff in the use of AI and *the creator has used AI to create, edit, revise and recreate the text that you see*. With that creation process clearly identified, let me explain the goals of this series.

Our Goals:

Credibility: Although AI has made — and continues to make — huge strides over the last few years, no unsupervised AI can create a truly reliable or fully credible college or seminary level text. The limitations of AI generated content sometimes originates from the limitations of the content itself (the training set may be inadequate), but more often, user dissatisfaction with AI-generated content arises from human errors associated with poor prompt engineering. The DTL Press has sought to overcome both of these problems by hiring established scholars with widely recognized expertise to create books within their areas of expertise and by training those scholars and experts in AI prompt engineering. To be clear, the scholar whose name appears on the cover of this work has created this volume — generating, reading, regenerating, rereading and revising the work. Even though the work was generated (in varying degrees) by AI, the names of our scholarly creators appear on the cover as a guarantee that the content is equally credible with any introductory work which that scholar/creator would pen using the traditional model.

Affordability: The DTL Press is committed to the idea that affordability should not be a barrier to knowledge. *All persons are equally deserving of the right to know and to understand.* Therefore, ebook versions of all DTL Press books are available from the DTL libraries without charge, and available as print books for a nominal fee. Our scholar/creators are to be thanked for their willingness to forego traditional royalty arrangements. (Our creators are compensated for their generative work, but they do not receive royalties in the traditional sense.)

Accessibility: The DTL Press would like to make high quality, low cost introductory textbooks available to everyone, everywhere in the world. The books in this series are immediately made available in multiple languages. The DTL Press will create translations in other languages upon request. Translations are, of course, generated by AI.

Our Acknowledged Limitations:

Some readers are undoubtedly thinking, "but AI can only produce derivative scholarship; AI can't create original, innovative scholarship." That criticism is, of course, largely accurate. AI is largely limited to aggregating, organizing and repackaging pre-existing ideas (although sometimes in ways that can be used to accelerate and refine the production of original scholarship). Still while acknowledging this inherent limitation of AI, the DTL Press would offer two comments: (1) Introductory texts are seldom meant to be truly ground breaking in their originality and (2) the DTL Press has other series dedicated to publishing original scholarship with traditional authorship.

Our Invitation:

The DTL Press would like to fundamentally reshape academic publishing in the theological world to make scholarship more accessible and more affordable in two ways. First, we would like to generate introductory texts in all areas of theological discourse, so that no one is ever forced to "buy a textbook" in any language. It is our vision for professors anywhere to be able to use one book, two books or an entire set of books in this series as the *introductory* textbooks for their classes. Second, we would also like to publish traditionally authored scholarly monographs for Open Access (free) distribution for an advanced scholarly readership.

Finally, the DTL Press is non-confessional and will publish works in any area of religious studies. Traditionally authored books are peer-reviewed; AI-generated introductory book creation is open to anyone with the required expertise to supervise content generation in that area of discourse. If you share the DTL Press's commitment to credibility, affordability and accessibility, contact us about changing the world of theological publishing by contributing to this series or a more traditionally authored series.

With high expectations,

Thomas E. Phillips

DTL Press Executive Director
www.thedtl.org

Author's Forward

AI is changing everything, even the incredibly change resistant ecologies of higher education and theological education. Although I possess neither a prophet's divinely inspired insight into the future nor a technologist's insider perspective on the next big thing, I think I do hold a position which should enable me to offer limited advice about AI to the curious, but largely uninitiated, theological educator.

Briefly, writing in the mode of Paul's "fool's speech" in 2 Corinthians, although I fully acknowledge the limits of my own comprehension and skills, I have more than a beginner's expertise in the two areas of discourse addressed in this little book. On the one hand, I have spent the last 3 decades in theological education, including two decades as a professor and scholar of the New Testament and another full decade as the executive director of the Digital Theological Library. I hold a Ph.D. in New Testament (SMU, 1998) and I have published widely in Biblical studies. On the other hand, I have a Masters in Information Systems (Drexel, 2012) and I have been deeply engaged with many global leaders in information technologies for the last several years. That ends the fool's speech.

Thus, I offer this book to theological educators as one who has one foot in theological education and perhaps one toe in the technology world. I offer this work *as advice from a novice to beginners*. Here's what I hope to accomplish with this book:

* Explain what AI is and how it works;
* Explain how leading academics and academic institutions are employing AI in the furtherance of their missions and work;
* Discuss some of the philosophical, ethical and theological issues associated with the existence and use of AI; and
* Provide some practical guidance about the use of AI.

I readily acknowledge that much of the book—particularly the more technical discussions—was composed with great assistance by AI (although I am fully accountable for every word in this book).

Many readers will find some sections of the book—particularly some of the earlier chapters about the technology of AI—rather etherical (perhaps downright perplexing) or perhaps even boring. *Readers who find themselves daydreaming their way through these earlier chapters are invited to skip ahead to the later, more practical and utilitarian, parts of the book.* Some readers will believe that I have "buried the lead"—or least delayed giving readers what they most need—until the end of the book. I can only give testimony to the fact that in my case, my use of AI has prompted an ever-increasing desire to understand how this stuff works so effectively. Then, my increasing understanding of AI has fueled a corresponding increase in my desire to master the use of this incredible technology. *The more I use AI, the more I want to understand AI. The more I understand AI, the more I want to use AI.*

Finally, let me add to this personal testimony by saying that the mission of the Digital Theological Library (DTL), which I am privileged to lead, is to *help everyone to engage in self-critical reflection upon their own faith and in humble dialogue with those of other traditions.* If you share regard for this mission, I am modestly confident—and quite hopeful—that you will find this book helpful. I am supremely confident that you will find AI helpful.

Thomas E. Phillips

(Traditionally authored)

Introduction
Why This Book Now?

Artificial intelligence is no longer a topic confined to computer science departments or Silicon Valley think tanks. It has entered the halls of our classrooms, the routines of our research, and the policies of our institutions. For educators and administrators working in spiritually-informed academic contexts, this emergence raises vital questions—not only about how we use AI, but about who we are becoming in its presence.

This book is written for those committed to the formation of people and communities through education grounded in spiritual values. Whether your institution is religiously affiliated, interfaith, or grounded in broader commitments to human dignity and ethical inquiry, you are likely already confronting the opportunities and tensions that AI presents.

You do not need to be a technologist to benefit from this work. If you care about education that nurtures the whole person—intellect, character, and spirit—then this guide is for you. Whether you are excited by innovation or wary of disruption, my hope is that these chapters will equip you to respond with clarity, wisdom, and purpose.

We stand at a cultural crossroads, where digital technologies and spiritual inquiry must speak to each other in new ways. May this book serve as a companion on that shared path.

Part I
Understanding Artificial Intelligence

Chapter 1
What Is AI and How Does It Work?

Artificial Intelligence (AI) has rapidly moved from the margins of technological development into the core of daily experience. Once the domain of speculative fiction or specialized research labs, AI now permeates the structures of education, communication, governance, and social interaction. In educational institutions shaped by spiritual values and commitments — whether rooted in particular religious traditions or more broadly in practices of meaning-making, discernment, and formation — this shift carries profound implications. *AI is not merely a tool; it is a complex phenomenon that reshapes the practices and purposes of learning.* It affects how we teach, how we evaluate, how we research, and even how we imagine the human mind and its relation to technology.

To begin this exploration, it is necessary to offer a clear and accessible account of what AI is and how it works. Although the field of AI is vast and technical in many of its dimensions, a foundational understanding can equip educators and institutional leaders to make informed, reflective, and ethically grounded decisions about its use. This chapter provides such an overview, emphasizing conceptual clarity over technical depth.

Artificial Intelligence refers broadly to the development of computer systems that can perform tasks traditionally associated with human intelligence. These tasks include processing language, identifying patterns, recognizing visual inputs, making data-driven predictions, and engaging in problem-solving activities.

While the phrase "artificial intelligence" may evoke images of sentient machines or human-like robots, contemporary AI systems do not possess consciousness, self-awareness, or intention. Rather, they simulate aspects of cognition through statistical modeling and computational power. They are tools—albeit extraordinarily powerful ones—that can emulate certain forms of learning, reasoning, and language generation.

Among the most significant developments in the contemporary landscape of AI is the rise of machine learning. Machine learning involves the use of algorithms that enable computers to detect patterns and improve their performance on specific tasks through exposure to data. Rather than following a rigid, pre-programmed set of instructions, machine learning systems adapt based on the information they process. One particular form of machine learning—known as deep learning—relies on artificial neural networks, which are loosely inspired by the structure of the human brain. These networks consist of layers of interconnected nodes through which data flows and is transformed, allowing the system to make increasingly accurate predictions or classifications.

Closely related to this development is the field of natural language processing (NLP), which focuses on enabling computers to understand, interpret, and generate human language. NLP powers a wide range of tools, from predictive text and language translation to conversational agents and writing assistants. One notable example is the large language model—such as the GPT series developed by OpenAI—which can generate coherent and contextually responsive text across a wide variety of topics. These generative models have become particularly influential in educational contexts, where they are used for content creation, language instruction, writing support, and administrative tasks.

While AI is often imagined in the abstract, it is already deeply embedded in everyday educational practices. Many learning management systems rely on AI to customize student experiences, automate grading, or identify at-risk learners. AI-driven applications assist with plagiarism detection, accessibility support (such as transcription or text-to-speech tools), and administrative forecasting. In more experimental contexts, educators are using AI to co-design syllabi, generate reading lists, and even simulate classroom dialogue. In short, AI is not a distant innovation—it is already reshaping the educational landscape, sometimes invisibly.

The expansion of AI into academic life brings both excitement and concern. On the one hand, these technologies offer unprecedented efficiencies, creative possibilities, and avenues for inclusion. They can reduce administrative burden, provide real-time feedback to students, and enhance multilingual engagement. On the other hand, the integration of AI raises serious ethical questions. Concerns about surveillance, bias, automation of judgment, and the erosion of personal interaction are increasingly urgent. In spiritually-oriented educational environments, such concerns take on even greater weight, as they intersect with questions about human dignity, moral agency, and the cultivation of wisdom.

From a spiritual perspective, AI also invites reflection on what it means to be human. If intelligence can be simulated, what distinguishes authentic understanding from patterned output? What is the role of intuition, empathy, and discernment—qualities that are often central to spiritual formation—in a context where machines appear to "learn" and "respond"?

These questions are not merely theoretical. They shape how educators frame learning outcomes, how institutions define integrity, and how communities of learning navigate the boundary between technological innovation and spiritual depth.

It is essential to recognize that AI systems are not neutral. They carry the imprint of their creators — their assumptions, values, and cultural biases. Algorithmic decisions often reflect larger patterns of inequality and exclusion, even when operating under the guise of objectivity. For educators committed to spiritual and ethical inquiry, this reality demands not only technical awareness but moral attentiveness. AI must be examined not simply for what it does, but for what it reveals about the systems and societies that produce it.

This book proceeds from the conviction that spiritual and ethical reflection must remain central to how we engage emerging technologies. The aim is not to reject AI, nor to embrace it uncritically, but to cultivate a posture of discerning engagement. In educational communities shaped by spiritual values — whether those values emerge from faith traditions, contemplative practices, or philosophical commitments to human flourishing — the questions surrounding AI must be addressed with courage, clarity, and compassion.

In the chapters that follow, we will examine specific applications of AI in teaching, research, institutional governance, and ethical reflection. This opening chapter has sought to lay the conceptual groundwork: to define artificial intelligence, to explain its basic mechanisms, and to begin to articulate the stakes involved in its use. AI is no longer optional. But the way we choose to understand and implement it remains open — and deeply consequential. As spiritually attentive educators, we are called not only to adapt to new tools, but to shape their use in light of the values we hold most dear.

Chapter 2
How a Large Language Model Is Made
The Development and Training of LLMs

While artificial intelligence is a broad and evolving field, the most transformative development impacting education today is the emergence of the Large Language Model, or LLM. These models — now integral to writing assistants, educational tools, research support systems, and conversational agents — are reshaping how educators engage language and information. In spiritually-informed institutions, where intellectual inquiry is intertwined with formative purpose, understanding how LLMs are created is essential for responsible engagement.

A Large Language Model is a type of artificial intelligence trained to generate and interpret natural human language. In essence, it functions as a probabilistic generator of words: given an initial text prompt, the model calculates what word (or fragment of a word) is statistically most likely to follow next, based on patterns learned from vast amounts of training data. *What makes a model "large" is twofold: first, the quantity and diversity of text data it processes, and second, the number of internal parameters — often in the billions — that it uses to make linguistic predictions.*

The development of an LLM begins with the collection of enormous datasets. These typically consist of publicly available text from books, websites, encyclopedias, social media, forums, and open educational resources. In many cases, the data spans multiple languages, genres, and disciplines, reflecting the messy complexity of human expression. However, this scale also introduces ethical risks. Since the data is scraped from the internet and other public sources, it can include biased, offensive, or misleading material. Such limitations are not simply technical—they are ethical and epistemological, and they matter deeply for institutions that ground education in spiritual responsibility.

Once a dataset has been compiled, it is processed through a series of steps to prepare it for training. This begins with cleaning—removing duplicate entries, stripping irrelevant content, correcting corrupt text, and normalizing punctuation and character sets. The text is then tokenized, meaning it is broken into smaller units that the model can manipulate. These units, called tokens, are typically whole words, sub-word segments, or symbols depending on the *tokenizer design*. For instance, the sentence "The spirit inspires learning" may be divided as shown in Figure 2.1.

Figure 2.1 — Tokenization of a Sample Sentence
Original Sentence: "The spirit inspires learning."
Tokenized: "The", "Ġspirit", "Ġinspires", "Ġlearning", "."

Figure 2.1. Tokenization breaks a sentence into units the model can understand. The symbol "Ġ" (a space indicator in Byte-Pair Encoding) shows where words begin. Less common words may be split further—for instance, "inspiration" might become ["Ġin", "spiration"].

Converting Tokens into Numbers
Once a sentence has been tokenized, the model cannot yet "understand" these tokens unless they are translated into numbers. Machine learning models process data mathematically, not linguistically. To bridge this gap, each token is mapped to a unique numerical identifier using a predefined vocabulary list.

This process is similar to assigning each word or word-piece an index in a very large dictionary. For example, the token "The" might be mapped to 4321, "Ġspirit" to 9823, and "." to 7. This mapping creates an input sequence of integers that can be fed into the model.

However, simple integer mapping is not enough. The model still needs a way to understand relationships between these numbers. To do this, each token's ID is passed through an embedding layer—a mathematical function that converts the integer into a high-dimensional vector. These vectors are designed so that semantically similar words are positioned close to each other in vector space. For example, the words "learning," "education," and "study" might end up clustered together, even though their original token IDs are arbitrary. The embedding space becomes a kind of conceptual map, built from statistical correlations in the training data.

Through this transformation, tokens go from being text strings → to indexed numbers → to numerical vectors. These vectors carry with them the statistical and contextual meaning of each token, enabling the model to compare them, weigh them, and make probabilistic predictions about which ones should follow in a given sequence.

Tokenization and embedding are foundational steps in the learning process. Once complete, these embeddings are passed into the model's architecture, which is typically based on the transformer—a neural network design introduced in 2017 that allows the model to attend to different parts of a sentence simultaneously. During training, the model receives a sequence of token embeddings and is tasked with predicting the next token in that sequence. For example, given the input "The spirit inspires," the model tries to guess that "learning" is the most likely next word. It does this through repeated trials, gradually adjusting internal parameters to reduce its prediction error. This optimization process, known as *gradient descent*, enables the model to improve its predictions over time by adjusting how it weighs various token relationships.

Figure 2.2 provides a simplified view of how a model processes text during training.

Figure 2.2 — Training Workflow in a Transformer-Based LLM

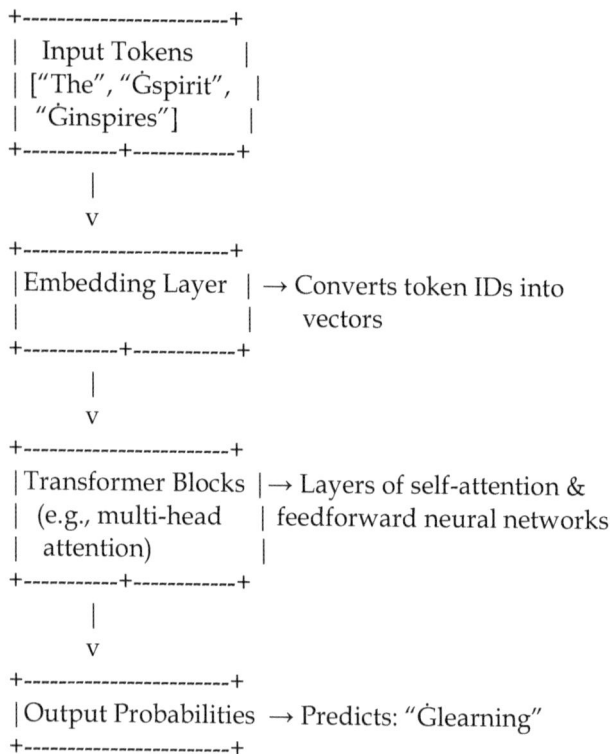

```
+------------------------+
|  Input Tokens          |
| ["The", "Ġspirit",     |
|  "Ġinspires"]          |
+-----------+------------+
     |
     v
+------------------------+
|Embedding Layer  | → Converts token IDs into
|                 |        vectors
+-----------+------------+
     |
     v
+------------------------+
|Transformer Blocks |→ Layers of self-attention &
| (e.g., multi-head  | feedforward neural networks
|   attention)       |
+-----------+------------+
     |
     v
+------------------------+
|Output Probabilities  → Predicts: "Ġlearning"
+------------------------+
```

Figure 2.2. A simplified representation of how a transformer model processes input during training. It uses an embedding layer to translate tokens into vectors, then passes them through transformer blocks, which adjust internal parameters to improve prediction accuracy.

This training process is repeated billions of times using powerful computing infrastructure and vast datasets. At the end of this phase, known as pretraining, the model is able to generate coherent and contextually responsive language across a wide variety of topics. However, it is still a general-purpose model at this stage and not yet optimized for interaction or specific tasks.

To refine its performance and align it more closely with human expectations, developers often apply a second phase called fine-tuning. This may involve training the model further on more curated, specialized datasets—such as academic texts, theological writings, or scientific literature. In many cases, a method known as Reinforcement Learning from Human Feedback (RLHF) is used. Here, human evaluators interact with the model, rank its outputs, and guide it toward more helpful, safe, or context-appropriate responses. This step is especially important in education, where nuance, tone, and clarity are critical.

The final model is then deployed to users through applications such as chatbots, writing assistants, search systems, or embedded tools in digital learning environments. While it may appear to "understand" language or "know" its subject, it is important to remember that the model lacks consciousness, intention, or spiritual awareness. It is not a sentient being, nor does it possess moral reasoning or epistemic humility. It responds to prompts by simulating language based on statistical probability—not through comprehension or conviction.

For spiritually attentive educators, this distinction is crucial. An LLM may generate a thoughtful reflection on love, justice, or the human condition, but it does so without feeling, belief, or discernment. It can mimic prayer or theological argument without engaging in any form of inner life or community accountability. Its brilliance is functional, not spiritual.

Nevertheless, these tools can be used thoughtfully and ethically within academic settings. They can support multilingual communication, accelerate administrative tasks, assist in curriculum design, and offer new modes of student engagement. However, their integration must be governed by spiritual values: care for the whole person, commitment to justice, discernment of truth, and humility in the face of mystery.

This chapter has introduced the process through which a Large Language Model is developed—from massive data collection and tokenization, through embedding, computational training, and human-guided fine-tuning. As we move to the next chapter, which examines how AI is currently being used in educational institutions around the world, this foundational understanding will serve as a guide. By demystifying how LLMs work, educators can better evaluate how and when to use them, and just as importantly, how to challenge and critique their limits in service to deeper educational and spiritual goals.

Chapter 3
AI in the World of Education and Scholarship

The rise of artificial intelligence is not a future event — it is a present and accelerating reality, already embedded in the infrastructure of higher education. From digital grading assistants and personalized learning platforms to research synthesis tools and virtual tutors, AI has begun to reshape how knowledge is transmitted, assessed, and even constructed. For educators, scholars, and institutional leaders working within spiritually-informed environments, these changes are not merely logistical. They are philosophical and formative, pressing us to reconsider how we teach, what we value, and how we support both learners and faculty in an age of intelligent machines.

This chapter surveys the current landscape of AI in education and scholarship. It identifies areas of integration, examines the benefits and limitations of emerging tools, and begins to articulate a spiritually grounded posture toward the use of AI in academic settings.

AI's Entrance into the Academy

Artificial intelligence entered educational systems through a gradual process, largely unnoticed by many outside the fields of educational technology and computer science. Recommendation systems in digital libraries, plagiarism detection tools, adaptive learning platforms, and grammar assistants like Grammarly have existed for years, powered by early forms of machine learning. What distinguishes the current moment is not only the sophistication of these tools but their generative and interactive capabilities. With the advent of large language models (LLMs) such as GPT-4, Claude, and Gemini, AI is now capable of producing original essays, answering complex questions, grading assignments, and engaging in sustained conversation. These models can simulate expertise across disciplines, offering plausible responses in the voice of a theologian, historian, philosopher, or scientist.

Many institutions have adopted these tools through educational platforms such as Duolingo, Khan Academy, and Coursera, all of which now incorporate AI to deliver personalized instruction and feedback. Some universities have begun piloting AI as administrative assistants, using chatbots to answer common questions, help with registration, or guide students through financial aid processes. Others are experimenting with AI to support curriculum development, especially for online or hybrid programs.

In scholarly research, AI is being used to scan and synthesize vast quantities of literature, identify trends across disciplines, suggest citations, and even generate initial drafts of academic prose. While these uses are still evolving and unevenly adopted, they signal a broader transformation: AI is becoming an intellectual partner in tasks previously reserved for human cognition.

Practical Benefits and Spiritual Opportunities
The integration of AI into education brings significant benefits. Chief among them is efficiency. AI tools can automate time-consuming tasks—such as grading, transcription, and formatting—freeing up faculty and staff for more relational and pedagogical

engagement. For educators who already bear administrative and teaching overloads, this automation can be deeply liberating.

Another major benefit is accessibility. AI-driven tools can support students with different learning needs and linguistic backgrounds. Automatic captioning, real-time translation, adaptive testing, and multimodal content creation allow institutions to reach more diverse learners with greater flexibility and personalization. Especially in global and interfaith educational settings, this accessibility aligns with spiritual commitments to inclusion, equity, and human dignity.

AI also opens creative possibilities. Professors can generate new teaching materials quickly, simulate opposing viewpoints in classroom debate, or collaborate with students to critique AI-generated summaries or interpretations. Used wisely, these tools can enhance active learning and critical thinking — not replace them.

For spiritually-informed institutions, these opportunities raise the question: How can AI be used not merely to deliver content, but to deepen formation? Might AI assist in creating reflective prompts, spiritual exercises, or multilingual meditations? Could it support ethical discussions, dialogue facilitation, or research in spiritual traditions from underrepresented communities?

The promise of AI, in this light, is not only technical. It can support a richer, more dialogical and inclusive vision of education — if guided by intentional values and spiritual imagination.

Risks, Limitations, and Misuses

Alongside its benefits, AI also brings significant risks — some technical, others ethical or spiritual in nature.

One major concern is bias. Because AI systems are trained on human-produced data, they often inherit the biases, exclusions, and prejudices embedded in that data. This can lead to distortions in outputs related to race, gender, religion, or cultural worldview. For educators and scholars in spiritually-rooted institutions, the uncritical adoption of such tools could subtly reinforce unjust narratives or epistemological imbalance.

Another risk is misinformation. LLMs generate plausible-sounding text, but they do not "know" whether what they generate is true. They may fabricate references, misrepresent arguments, or invent historical details with confidence. For students — especially those unfamiliar with the material — these errors can go undetected. For faculty, this means that any use of AI-generated text must be accompanied by rigorous human verification.

More broadly, there is the danger of intellectual dependency. If students become overly reliant on AI to summarize texts, complete readings, or draft assignments, they risk outsourcing their interpretive and critical faculties. This diminishes not only academic integrity but the deeper formation of character, judgment, and reflective awareness — hallmarks of spiritually-grounded education.

There is also a more subtle concern: the erosion of relationality. Education, at its best, is a human exchange — a meeting of minds and hearts. The widespread substitution of AI for teacher feedback, peer collaboration, or contemplative processing may fragment the holistic nature of learning. A student might receive fast and fluent responses from an AI tutor, but those responses are void of empathy, intuition, or spiritual presence.

Toward a Spiritually Grounded Posture

How, then, should spiritually-oriented institutions respond? The task is not to reject AI outright, nor to accept it uncritically. It is to adopt a posture of informed discernment.

This posture begins with awareness: understanding how AI tools function, where they draw their knowledge from, and what limitations they carry. Educators must be willing to interrogate the design of the systems they use, to ask whose voices are centered, whose are omitted, and what epistemologies are encoded in the data. A spiritually grounded pedagogy insists that means matter, not just outcomes.

Second, discernment involves policy. Institutions must articulate clear guidelines about the appropriate use of AI in teaching, learning, and scholarship. These policies should be shaped not only by concerns about academic honesty but by questions of formation, justice, and well-being.

Finally, a spiritually grounded approach seeks possibility within limits. AI can never replace the spiritual mentor, the wise guide, or the discerning community. But it may serve as a tool in their service — providing structure, inspiration, and new pathways for reflection. The challenge is to integrate it in ways that remain true to the deeper aims of education: the pursuit of wisdom, the cultivation of compassion, and the transformation of the learner.

Conclusion

Artificial intelligence is now an active participant in the world of education and scholarship. Its influence is already visible — in workflows, platforms, administrative systems, and intellectual tools. For spiritually attentive educators, this is not a moment for panic, nor for passive adoption. It is a moment for thoughtful leadership.

This chapter has offered a survey of how AI is being used across educational settings, highlighting both its benefits and its risks. The chapters that follow will explore specific domains where AI can support teaching, learning, and research in more detail. Throughout, our guiding question remains the same: How might this technology serve the formation of whole persons in the context of spiritual and ethical education?

Part II
AI in Theological
and Academic Work

Chapter 4
AI for Classroom Preparation

In spiritually-formed education, teaching is understood not merely as the transfer of information, but as a formative and relational vocation. It encompasses intellectual inquiry, ethical discernment, and the shaping of the whole person. While much attention is paid to the moment of instruction, the work of preparation—developing syllabi, selecting readings, designing assignments, and structuring content—plays an equally essential role. It is in preparation that the educator meditates on the learning process, discerning how best to cultivate wisdom, curiosity, and integrity among students.

As artificial intelligence becomes increasingly integrated into educational practice, it now enters this preparatory space. The question is not simply whether such tools will be used, but how they will be used. Specifically, educators must ask whether AI can assist in ways that enhance rather than diminish the formative dimensions of teaching. Can it serve the work of design without short-circuiting discernment? Might it support educators in crafting thoughtful, responsive courses that are anchored in spiritual tradition and ethical rigor?

The design of a syllabus is among the most intellectually and spiritually intensive forms of academic labor. It is not a neutral roadmap but a document that expresses educational philosophy, theological orientation, and institutional mission. In settings where Scripture, theological reflection, and historical texts form the backbone of the curriculum, designing a syllabus often involves balancing ancient sources with contemporary applications, doctrinal concerns with practical wisdom, and foundational beliefs with critical inquiry.

AI tools, particularly large language models, can assist educators at this early stage. Given a course title and general theme — such as "Forgiveness and Justice in the Prophetic Tradition" — a language model can generate a preliminary course outline, suggest weekly topics, and propose learning objectives. It might also recommend readings from major theological voices, key biblical passages, and secondary sources. In this way, the educator receives a scaffold from which to build, revise, and personalize.

More advanced applications involve aligning learning outcomes with appropriate assessments. If a desired outcome is for students to "evaluate contrasting interpretations of atonement in early ecclesial texts," AI may suggest written comparisons, student-led dialogues, or group case studies grounded in particular scriptural episodes such as the parable of the prodigal son or the Passion narratives. Language models can also produce draft rubrics, identify potential challenges, and recommend assignment sequences to support scaffolded learning across a term.

Beyond individual courses, AI can aid in curriculum mapping. An instructor revising a course on New Testament ethics might input a series of syllabi and ask the model to identify overlap, underrepresentation of certain themes (e.g., poverty, gender, eschatology), or opportunities for integration with other disciplines, such as historical theology or pastoral care. Such assistance may be particularly valuable for newer faculty or for institutions engaged in comprehensive curriculum review.

Despite these affordances, it is essential to emphasize that a syllabus is not a mechanical artifact. It is an expression of pedagogical identity. In many spiritually-formed institutions, it is crafted in light of communal identity, institutional calling, and a theological anthropology that regards students as bearers of divine image and potential. AI cannot capture this depth. Its suggestions must be interpreted, reworked, and filtered through the educator's discernment, tradition, and vision of what constitutes formative learning.

In addition to syllabi, educators must often prepare lecture materials: outlines, presentations, handouts, and thematic explorations. Here, AI tools can provide inspiration and structure. For example, an instructor preparing a session on the Sermon on the Mount might prompt an AI system to generate an overview of the Beatitudes, draw comparisons with parallel teachings in prophetic literature, or suggest modern applications in relation to justice, nonviolence, and mercy. AI can also assist in adapting material to multiple levels of complexity. A passage like Romans 5 could be summarized for first-year undergraduates, expanded for advanced exegesis courses, or translated into discussion prompts for adult learners engaged in spiritual formation.

Moreover, AI can support the identification of key theological tensions or interpretive challenges. In a lecture on divine judgment and mercy, for instance, AI could provide sample student objections, misreadings, or contemporary analogies that the instructor may wish to address. It may also suggest scriptural or doctrinal counterpoints—for example, setting the flood narrative in Genesis alongside the covenantal promises of Isaiah, or exploring how themes of retributive and restorative justice play out across testaments.

Still, these tools must be handled with caution. Language models do not understand the gravity or sanctity of the materials they process. They may confuse figures, misrepresent doctrines, or draw on sources with subtle but meaningful distortions. They may, for instance, conflate the Johannine and Synoptic portrayals of Jesus without regard to theological intent, or treat apocalyptic literature as merely symbolic without grappling with its historical and eschatological dimensions. It is the educator's responsibility to correct such errors, to preserve the richness and integrity of the tradition being taught, and to ensure that the use of AI does not flatten spiritual depth into mere data.

AI can also be enlisted in creating assignments, reflection prompts, and classroom exercises. For example, an instructor leading a course on Pauline theology might ask AI to generate case studies illustrating real-life ethical dilemmas addressed in 1 Corinthians. Alternatively, a course on biblical justice might draw on AI-generated scenarios that invite students to compare the ethical demands of the Law with those in the teachings of Jesus. In a homiletics course, AI might generate contrasting sermon outlines on a single passage, encouraging students to evaluate theological coherence, exegetical faithfulness, and rhetorical effectiveness.

Used well, these applications foster engagement and creativity. But without oversight, they risk trivializing sacred content or reinforcing cultural and theological biases. A prompt on discipleship, for instance, might yield material that emphasizes individualistic themes over communal ones, or that mirrors only one strand of theological interpretation. The instructor's role is again central: not to outsource pedagogy, but to deepen and contextualize it through critical use of AI.

One of the most practical uses of AI in the preparatory phase is in multilingual and multimodal support. For institutions with diverse student populations, AI can translate course materials, summarize complex readings, or produce audio versions of lectures. These affordances can make courses more accessible, reduce cognitive load, and support inclusive pedagogy. For example, a student reading Matthew 25 in a second language might benefit from an AI-generated glossary of terms, a historical overview of eschatological parables, or a visual timeline of related themes. In this way, AI can extend the hospitality of the classroom to those whose engagement may otherwise be constrained by language or format.

Still, spiritual teaching depends on more than clarity. It also depends on depth, nuance, and resonance. Translation tools may mishandle doctrinal vocabulary or overlook the emotional register of lament and praise. Simplified summaries may fail to convey the rhetorical force of prophetic or epistolary literature. The educator must therefore attend not only to accessibility but to fidelity—ensuring that what is shared retains the capacity to challenge, convict, and transform.

Ultimately, the use of AI in classroom preparation invites a renewed commitment to discernment. These technologies are not replacements for educators, but tools that require guidance. Their value lies not in what they can do, but in how thoughtfully they are used. The preparation of a course remains a deeply human and spiritual act. It involves prayerful reflection, cultural attentiveness, pedagogical skill, and theological imagination. In this light, AI may serve not as a substitute but as a support—a resource to prompt new thinking, extend one's reach, and conserve time for the work that only the educator can do.

Artificial intelligence can assist with many aspects of classroom preparation — from syllabus design and lecture development to assignment creation and linguistic accessibility. But its use must be shaped by the educator's commitment to thoughtful, spiritually grounded pedagogy. Preparation is not merely a technical task. It is a form of care for the learning environment, a setting of the table for wisdom to be encountered. Used well, AI may help set the table more fully; but it cannot serve the meal.

The next chapter will turn from preparation to practice, exploring how AI can function in the active dynamics of teaching and learning. There, too, the challenge will be to preserve the integrity of the educational relationship and the depth of formation, even as we make space for technological assistance.

Chapter 5
AI in Teaching and Learning

The act of teaching is never reducible to the delivery of content. It is a relational encounter shaped by shared inquiry, formative dialogue, and the cultivation of moral and intellectual character. In settings where the goal of education extends beyond knowledge acquisition to include spiritual discernment and ethical development, the classroom becomes a space not only of cognition but of transformation. Within this context, the emergence of artificial intelligence into the live setting of teaching and learning raises profound questions: How can educators make use of AI without displacing the essential human dynamics of instruction? What kinds of learning does AI foster or hinder? And in what ways might it serve, if properly directed, the deeper purposes of formation?

Artificial intelligence now enters the classroom in multiple forms. Language models embedded in chatbots provide students with instant explanations of complex ideas. Adaptive learning platforms adjust content in real time to match student performance. AI-generated simulations offer immersive case studies or historical reconstructions. Even in traditional settings, students may use AI tools outside of class to supplement reading, generate study notes, or draft reflections. These developments are reshaping the experience of learning in real time.

Among the most widespread uses of AI in teaching is its function as a tutoring or dialogue partner. Students can pose questions to a model about a biblical passage, a doctrinal debate, or a historical figure and receive a relatively coherent response. A student reading the opening chapters of Genesis might ask about differing interpretations of the creation narratives and receive a summary distinguishing between literalist, poetic, and theological readings. Similarly, a student preparing a paper on Augustine's view of grace might receive a synthesized account of key themes in *Confessions* and *On Nature and Grace*, along with suggestions for further inquiry. For students who are shy, uncertain, or new to theological language, such access can provide confidence and momentum. It may allow for a kind of exploratory rehearsal before entering the more communal and accountable space of classroom discussion.

This availability of responsive dialogue also enables greater flexibility. In asynchronous or hybrid courses, AI tools can serve as supplemental tutors, offering clarifications or rephrasing complex material. For example, a student struggling to grasp the nuances of Paul's argument in Romans might ask an AI to simplify the flow of reasoning in chapters 5 through 8. In turn, the model could offer a step-by-step breakdown of the contrast between death in Adam and life in the Messiah, or between law and grace, using metaphors and examples appropriate to the learner's context.

However, while these interactions can support comprehension, they also risk substituting mechanical fluency for contemplative depth. Language models generate text based on probabilities, not on conviction or understanding. They do not know the texts they interpret. They do not pray the psalms, nor wrestle with the Beatitudes. They can simulate theological conversation, but they cannot participate in it. In spiritually formed education, where formation is not only intellectual but dispositional, such distinctions are not optional. They are essential.

Moreover, educators must be attentive to the shape of the learning that AI encourages. Because AI systems are designed to produce fluent, confident responses, they may foster a mode of inquiry that privileges speed over patience and clarity over complexity. In matters of faith, doctrine, and history, such tendencies are dangerous. For example, when asked about the nature of atonement, an AI may present penal substitution as a singular or dominant interpretation without acknowledging alternative views such as moral influence or *Christus Victor*. Likewise, a query about the book of Revelation may yield an eschatological timeline but omit pastoral, liturgical, or anti-imperial readings that are vital to a fuller understanding. The educator's task, then, is to model and require a more critical engagement—one that recognizes the partiality of AI-generated content and returns students to sources, traditions, and conversations that exceed the model's outputs.

There are also concerns about how AI may shape the social dynamics of the classroom. When students grow accustomed to receiving instant, seemingly authoritative answers from non-human systems, their disposition toward communal inquiry may shift. The dialogical nature of learning—the give-and-take of interpretation, the humility of listening, the discernment that emerges in shared silence—can be weakened. This is especially true when engagement with sacred texts becomes mediated by tools that have no spiritual posture, no reverence, no community, and no memory. The danger is not merely distraction, but deformation: the gradual substitution of surface understanding for inward transformation.

Yet, AI can also be used to enrich dialogue when employed with intention. Educators might use AI-generated materials as starting points for critical response. A professor might assign students to evaluate a model's interpretation of the parable of the Good Samaritan, asking them to identify theological omissions, cultural assumptions, or rhetorical strategies. In another context, students might compare AI-generated summaries of major councils with original conciliar texts, noting what is preserved, distorted, or elided. Such exercises can develop critical literacy and deepen respect for the complexity of theological and historical discourse.

AI can also facilitate collaborative learning. In group settings, students might use AI to generate contrasting perspectives on a passage — such as the command to turn the other cheek in the Sermon on the Mount — and then discuss the ethical and practical implications of each reading. In preaching courses, students might evaluate AI-generated homiletic outlines and rewrite them in light of their community's needs and spiritual convictions. Used in this way, AI becomes a foil rather than an authority — a tool to sharpen awareness, not to dictate meaning.

One of the more promising dimensions of AI in the classroom is its capacity to support differentiated learning. Not all students arrive with the same background in Scripture, doctrine, or historical theology. Some may come from traditions steeped in liturgical life; others from more spontaneous or rationalist contexts; still others from experiences marked by silence, trauma, or exclusion. AI can offer personalized support by rephrasing content, supplying context, or suggesting further readings appropriate to a learner's prior knowledge. A student unfamiliar with the synoptic problem, for instance, may use AI to learn the basic outlines of source criticism before engaging in classroom analysis of the Gospels. Another student, encountering the rule of Benedict for the first time, might prompt AI to explain its spiritual logic in contemporary terms.

Nonetheless, personalization must not become isolation. Spiritual learning depends on community. It involves being seen, heard, and challenged. The teacher's task is to accompany students through uncertainty, to bear witness to struggle, to affirm growth that is often invisible to the student themselves. No AI can perform these functions. No model can offer pastoral care, respond to tears, or speak a word of wisdom at the right time. These are the tasks of the educator — not because they are more emotional or humane, but because they are relational, covenantal, and responsive to the living presence of others.

The role of the educator, then, is not eclipsed by AI. It is clarified. Teachers must become more deliberate in cultivating presence, more reflective in modeling humility, and more courageous in holding space for questions that do not yield to immediate answers. They must help students see technology not as a source of wisdom but as a tool to be tested and interpreted. In doing so, they help learners develop not only intellectual competence, but spiritual maturity.

Artificial intelligence will continue to shape the landscape of teaching and learning. It will become more embedded, more invisible, more persuasive. For educators working within traditions rooted in Scripture, prayer, and communal discernment, this context demands clarity of purpose. The classroom is not a place to compete with technology. It is a place to form persons — thoughtful, attentive, and wise. When used with care, AI may support this work. But it can never define it.

The following chapter will explore how AI can assist with academic research, including literature review, translation, bibliographic tools, and data analysis. As with teaching, the guiding concern will remain the same: how to use these technologies in ways that honor the intellectual and spiritual aims of education.

Chapter 6
AI for Academic Research

Academic research is a vital dimension of spiritually-informed education. It sustains the intellectual depth of teaching, supports the development of theological and ethical reflection, and preserves the wisdom of tradition for future generations. In institutions shaped by scriptural engagement, historical consciousness, and doctrinal inquiry, research is not pursued as an abstract exercise, but as a calling — rooted in the conviction that truth-seeking, when rightly directed, is a form of devotion.

The emergence of artificial intelligence into the research process represents a major shift in how scholarly work is conceived and conducted. Large language models and related AI tools now offer new capacities for retrieving, organizing, summarizing, translating, and even generating scholarly content. These capabilities have the potential to support and accelerate the research process, especially for scholars working under time constraints, in under-resourced contexts, or across multiple linguistic and disciplinary boundaries. Yet they also raise critical concerns regarding reliability, authorship, epistemic integrity, and the preservation of contemplative rigor in theological inquiry.

This chapter explores the use of AI in academic research within spiritually-attuned environments. It considers the possibilities AI opens for literature review, bibliographic exploration, summarization, translation, and data analysis, while highlighting the discernments necessary to ensure that such tools serve rather than distort the aims of research grounded in tradition, wisdom, and moral accountability.

One of the most immediate applications of AI in research is the task of conducting literature reviews. When scholars begin writing on a topic — such as divine justice in the prophetic tradition, the theology of the body in Pauline letters, or the development of monastic spirituality in late antiquity — they must first map the landscape of existing scholarship. This involves identifying key texts, tracing interpretive trajectories, and discerning gaps or tensions in the field. AI tools can assist in this process by generating overviews, locating citations, and clustering themes across disciplines. When prompted with a question about the interpretation of Psalm 22 across patristic and medieval sources, for example, an AI model might supply summaries of early commentary traditions, note variations in Christological emphasis, and point to relevant secondary literature.

These tools can be especially helpful in interdisciplinary or cross-cultural research, where unfamiliarity with a parallel field or region may present obstacles. A scholar exploring ecclesial responses to poverty might use AI to trace how economic themes in Acts are interpreted in Latin American liberation theology, North African homiletics, and early Syriac monasticism. AI can surface threads that might otherwise remain buried in footnotes, untranslated articles, or underindexed journals.

However, literature review tools driven by AI also present limitations. Because language models generate text based on patterns in their training data, they may fabricate citations, conflate interpretations, or omit marginal voices. For instance, when asked for sources on the role of women in early church leadership, an AI model may reproduce dominant Eurocentric perspectives while ignoring non-Western or non-canonical sources. Moreover, the apparent fluency of AI-generated summaries can obscure the fact that they are not grounded in critical judgment, but in algorithmic prediction. This creates the risk that scholars — especially those new to a topic — may confuse convenience with comprehension.

To mitigate this risk, *AI tools must be treated as heuristic aids rather than definitive authorities.* The researcher's task remains one of verification, evaluation, and interpretation. AI can assist with breadth, but depth requires human discernment, contextual sensitivity, and spiritual attentiveness. In theological inquiry especially, where nuance and tradition matter profoundly, the synthetic summaries of AI must be tested against careful reading, lived community, and dialogical engagement.

Another area where AI can assist research is in bibliographic organization. Applications now exist that can analyze a corpus of documents, extract references, categorize them by theme or period, and generate annotated bibliographies or reading lists. For scholars writing dissertations, book chapters, or grant proposals, such functionality can save significant time and help identify overlooked connections. For example, a scholar preparing a project on asceticism and embodiment in late antiquity might use AI to generate a comparative list of primary texts (e.g., *The Life of Antony, Sayings of the Desert Fathers*) alongside modern commentaries, theological analyses, and anthropological critiques.

This capacity can be extended through citation management tools that now integrate AI features. These tools can suggest formatting corrections, detect inconsistencies, or recommend additional sources based on existing citations. Such tools, if used carefully, can support clarity and thoroughness. Yet here too, they require oversight. AI cannot determine the theological weight of a citation or discern the pastoral significance of a footnote. Only the scholar, situated in a specific intellectual and spiritual community, can do that.

Translation is another domain where AI shows considerable promise. Multilingual research is often limited by language barriers, especially when working with sources in Greek, Latin, Syriac, or modern non-English languages. AI-based translation tools can offer draft translations of theological texts, ecclesiastical documents, or historical records, enabling initial access where otherwise there would be none. A researcher exploring early North African theology, for instance, might use AI to translate sermons from Augustine or Cyprian that remain untranslated, or to access contemporary scholarship in French or Portuguese.

However, theological translation is not a simple matter of word substitution. It requires sensitivity to spiritual tone, doctrinal precision, and cultural resonance. The term "logos," for example, cannot be rendered merely as "word" without considering its philosophical and theological implications across Johannine literature and early creedal development. Likewise, idiomatic expressions of lament, praise, or mystery — found in scriptural texts or spiritual poetry — often resist literal or mechanical rendering. AI translations, while useful as a starting point, must be checked against existing scholarly translations, lexical tools, and contextual knowledge.

AI can also assist with data analysis in research projects that involve patterns, statistics, or textual corpora. For example, a scholar analyzing rhetorical patterns in Pauline epistles might use AI to track the frequency of certain ethical exhortations across different letters, or to visualize how metaphors of light and darkness function in sapiential literature. Digital humanities projects increasingly rely on such tools to code themes, map networks, and detect shifts in theological language across time or geography.

In some contexts, AI has also been used to assist in manuscript comparison, identifying variant readings, stylistic interpolations, or scribal trends across large textual datasets. These tools can enrich the field of textual criticism, especially when combined with traditional philological training. Nevertheless, the interpretation of these patterns remains a human task — one shaped by theological imagination, historical knowledge, and scholarly humility.

Throughout all these applications, a consistent principle emerges: AI can enhance research when it is embedded within a larger framework of critical, spiritually grounded scholarship. It cannot replace careful reading, community dialogue, spiritual reflection, or theological intuition. Indeed, its very speed and breadth can tempt scholars toward premature conclusions, reducing the labor of interpretation to the aggregation of sources. In traditions that prize wisdom over information, formation over accumulation, this is a temptation that must be resisted.

Research is not only about producing knowledge. It is also about stewarding traditions, interrogating assumptions, and contributing to the moral and spiritual life of communities. The scholar, in this view, is not a content generator, but a servant of understanding — tasked with holding together mystery and meaning, past and present, contemplation and critique. AI may assist in this task, but it must never define it.

This chapter has explored the uses and limits of AI in academic research: how it may support literature reviews, bibliographies, translation, and analysis, and how it must be integrated with care and discernment. The next chapter will consider how AI affects the evaluation of student work, and how institutions and educators might assess learning in ways that preserve academic integrity and spiritual formation in an age of intelligent machines.

Chapter 7
Evaluating Students in the Age of AI

Assessment is a central element of the educational process. It not only measures learning but shapes it. What educators choose to evaluate, and how they evaluate it, reveals their understanding of what matters in the classroom and beyond. In spiritually-informed institutions, assessment is not simply a means of ranking or certifying students; it is part of a broader commitment to formation. Evaluating student work involves attention to growth in wisdom, character, and understanding, not just mastery of content.

The arrival of artificial intelligence into the academic landscape has introduced new complexities to the task of evaluation. Students now have access to tools that can generate essays, summarize texts, solve problems, and simulate scholarly analysis. These tools, while potentially useful for study and synthesis, also raise concerns about authorship, integrity, and the formation of intellectual virtue. Educators must now ask whether a given piece of student work reflects genuine engagement, and how to assess learning in a context where artificial assistance is often invisible, and at times indistinguishable from human effort.

This chapter explores the implications of AI for student evaluation. It addresses both practical and philosophical questions: How can educators ensure fairness and accuracy in grading? How can institutions promote integrity without resorting to surveillance or suspicion? And how might evaluation practices be reimagined to emphasize discernment, reflection, and transformation, rather than replication of information?

One of the most pressing concerns related to AI and student evaluation is the potential for plagiarism or unauthorized assistance. Language models can now generate entire essays on topics such as the theology of suffering in Job, the ethics of wealth in Luke's Gospel, or the meaning of sacrificial love in the writings of Paul. These essays often appear coherent, well-structured, and stylistically appropriate. They may even include footnotes and references, some real and some fabricated. For instructors reading dozens of submissions, the presence of such material can be difficult to detect.

Various software tools now claim to detect AI-generated content, analyzing patterns of vocabulary, sentence structure, and probability. However, these tools are not fully reliable. They may produce false positives, misidentify student writing styles, or be circumvented by paraphrasing software. Moreover, reliance on detection software can create an adversarial dynamic between students and educators, undermining the atmosphere of trust and respect that is essential to spiritually grounded learning.

In light of these challenges, many educators are reconsidering the nature and purpose of assessment. Rather than relying primarily on traditional take-home essays or online quizzes—formats most susceptible to AI assistance—they are turning to assignments that require personal reflection, contextual interpretation, and dialogical engagement. For example, instead of asking students to summarize the theology of the cross in 1 Corinthians, a professor might invite them to reflect on how Paul's message of weakness and power speaks to contemporary forms of ministry, injustice, or reconciliation. Responses that integrate lived experience, class discussion, and community context are more difficult to generate artificially and more likely to reflect authentic learning.

Similarly, oral exams, in-class writing exercises, collaborative projects, and creative presentations offer opportunities for real-time assessment of student understanding. These formats invite students to speak in their own voice, respond to follow-up questions, and demonstrate the integration of knowledge and interpretation. A classroom discussion on Matthew 25, for instance, might ask students to compare the parable of the sheep and the goats with local expressions of hospitality or community service, fostering both biblical literacy and ethical imagination.

Rubrics can also be adjusted to reward originality, depth of insight, and engagement with primary sources. In place of purely analytic criteria, educators might emphasize interpretive nuance, theological coherence, or practical application. A homiletics course might assess not only the structure of a sermon but the extent to which it reflects prayerful preparation, contextual relevance, and pastoral sensitivity. A course on early councils might ask students to write a fictional pastoral letter from a historical figure, articulating the implications of Nicene Christology for contemporary questions of identity and suffering.

In addition to rethinking assignments, institutions must cultivate cultures of integrity that go beyond rules and penalties. Students should be invited into conversations about why honesty matters—not only because deception leads to unfair grades, but because it undermines the very process of formation. When students present ideas that are not their own, they lose the opportunity to wrestle, question, and grow. They short-circuit the slow work of insight, and with it, the spiritual humility that comes from acknowledging one's limits and seeking truth in community.

Such conversations are best conducted not as disciplinary interventions but as part of the educational journey itself. Faculty might begin a semester by discussing the value of original work, the appropriate use of technological tools, and the spiritual disciplines of reading, writing, and critical engagement. Course policies should be transparent, reasonable, and framed not as constraints but as invitations to integrity.

At the institutional level, codes of conduct and academic integrity statements should be revisited in light of emerging technologies. Rather than focusing only on prohibition, these documents might articulate shared commitments to truthfulness, accountability, and the flourishing of others. A statement on academic honesty might affirm that the pursuit of knowledge is also a spiritual practice—one that demands attention, patience, and care. Policies can also clarify expectations around the use of AI: when it is permissible, how it should be cited, and what forms of assistance constitute misrepresentation.

Importantly, educators should model the practices they seek to cultivate. When faculty engage with AI tools in their own work—using them for editing, summarization, or organization—they can share this process with students, demonstrating how to use such tools ethically and transparently. They can also acknowledge their own questions and uncertainties, fostering a shared ethos of exploration rather than control.

Some educators may fear that the widespread availability of AI will make deep learning impossible. But such a conclusion is premature. While AI can simulate certain forms of knowledge, it cannot replicate wisdom, discernment, or transformation. These are the deeper aims of education in spiritually-informed institutions. When evaluation focuses not merely on correct answers but on thoughtful process — on the ability to listen, interpret, and respond with care — it creates space for genuine learning. AI may influence the form of assessment, but it need not displace its purpose.

The challenge, then, is to design assignments and assessments that are not only difficult to automate but also worth doing. These are the kinds of tasks that engage the whole person: exercises in theological imagination, ethical reflection, communal dialogue, and the application of faith to life. In a course on prayer, for example, a final assignment might ask students to write and annotate a personal rule of life grounded in biblical and historical sources. In a seminar on the early church, students might be asked to design a catechetical curriculum for a modern faith community, drawing on ancient texts and contemporary challenges. Such assignments resist plagiarism not through surveillance but by inviting authenticity.

Evaluation, at its best, is not punitive but formative. It seeks not to catch students in error but to accompany them in growth. In a world where machines can generate text, what becomes most valuable is the voice that cannot be replicated — the voice shaped by study, prayer, dialogue, and conviction. Educators have the responsibility to nurture that voice, and assessment remains one of the ways in which it is heard, tested, and refined.

The next chapter will extend the conversation into broader institutional and ethical territory. It will ask how schools, departments, and faculties can approach AI strategically and responsibly — crafting policies, fostering faculty development, and preparing for a future in which discernment and imagination will be more necessary than ever.

Part III
Ethical, Theological, and Institutional Considerations

Chapter 8
AI and Copyright Law
Training, Ownership, and the Boundaries of Expression

The rapid integration of artificial intelligence into the academic and creative landscape has raised serious questions about intellectual property, particularly in the realms of authorship, originality, and the reuse of existing content. As AI systems become more deeply embedded in theological research, publishing, and teaching, institutions are being forced to confront the legal and ethical frameworks that shape how these technologies can and should be used. Central to this discussion are two legal principles that, taken together, help define the boundaries of lawful and responsible AI development: the doctrine of transformative use, and the foundational rule that ideas themselves cannot be copyrighted.

At the heart of the current legal debate is the question of whether training AI models on copyrighted materials constitutes infringement. Large language models (LLMs), such as those that power advanced conversational systems, are trained on massive corpora of text—including books, academic articles, websites, and theological resources—many of which are under copyright protection. Developers of these systems argue that the process of training is fundamentally transformative. The AI does not store or reproduce texts verbatim; rather, it uses the patterns and structures found in these texts to generate new and unpredictable outputs. In this view, training is not about copying but about learning, not about exploitation but about synthesis.

The concept of transformative use is central to this defense. In U.S. copyright law, fair use allows certain unauthorized uses of copyrighted works when the new use adds new expression, meaning, or purpose. Courts have historically recognized transformative use in contexts such as parody, commentary, and search engine indexing. AI developers argue that training constitutes a similar transformation. The purpose of the original text may have been doctrinal instruction or historical commentary, while the purpose of training is to enable general linguistic reasoning across an array of subjects. The function, intent, and impact are different.

Whether this argument will prevail is not yet clear. Multiple lawsuits are pending in the United States and elsewhere, brought by authors, visual artists, news organizations, and software developers who contend that AI companies have built commercial tools on the unpaid labor of human creators. Some critics argue that AI systems are now capable of generating outputs that directly compete with the works from which they learned, raising questions about whether the use is truly transformative or merely derivative. Courts will eventually need to assess whether the training of AI models sufficiently transforms the underlying materials to justify exemption from liability. These cases will likely define the future legal contours of AI development and fair use.

European Union law, by contrast, is more structured in its limitations. Under the 2019 EU Copyright Directive, certain forms of text and data mining are permitted for research and innovation, but rightsholders may opt out by explicitly denying consent for such uses. This has led to mounting pressure for AI developers to maintain transparency regarding the data used in training and to seek licenses or permissions where necessary. While such regulation might protect creators, it also raises concerns about restricting access to broad-based educational content — an issue particularly relevant in theology, where many foundational ideas are centuries old and culturally pervasive.

Alongside the question of training data, a second pressing issue concerns the ownership and copyright status of AI-generated outputs. Who, if anyone, owns the text produced by an AI when it is prompted by a user? Can such material be copyrighted, or is it inherently outside the scope of legal protection?

Under current law in most jurisdictions, copyright applies only to works of human authorship. AI-generated outputs that are produced without meaningful human input are not eligible for protection. The U.S. Copyright Office, for instance, has made clear that works created entirely by AI systems cannot be registered as copyrighted property. However, when human users direct, edit, or reshape the outputs in substantial ways, there may be grounds for partial or full copyright attribution. The line between assisted and authored work remains blurry, and institutions will need to establish their own policies for evaluating and disclosing AI involvement in publications, assignments, and teaching materials.

These issues lead naturally into a related and often misunderstood area of copyright law: the distinction between ideas and expressions. One of the bedrock principles of intellectual property is that ideas are not protected by copyright. Only the specific way an idea is expressed — through wording, structure, style, or form — is eligible for legal protection. This doctrine preserves the open exchange of knowledge and ensures that no single person or group can claim exclusive rights over theological concepts, historical claims, or ethical frameworks. It is the formulation, not the idea itself, that is protected.

This distinction is critically important in the AI context. During training, AI models absorb patterns of association, syntax, and meaning from vast quantities of text. But they do not (except in rare and unintended cases) memorize or reproduce specific phrasings. Instead, they develop a probabilistic understanding of how words relate to one another based on observed usage. Thus, when a model generates a paragraph about divine providence, it is not retrieving a stored quote from Thomas Aquinas or Karl Barth; it is generating a new formulation of an old idea. Since ideas cannot be copyrighted, and since the generated output is not a copy of a protected expression, the legal claim of infringement becomes more difficult to sustain — so long as the model avoids close paraphrase or unattributed reproduction.

This framework helps reassure educators and researchers who rely on AI tools to support thinking, drafting, or teaching. The fact that AI may have been trained on copyrighted theological literature does not, by itself, make the use of the tool unlawful — particularly when the user is generating new material, contributing original thought, and applying it within an educational or scholarly context. However, users should still be cautious. It is best to avoid using AI to summarize or rewrite entire copyrighted articles, especially without attribution. When in doubt, cite sources, disclose AI involvement, and review output carefully for unintentional replication.

Ultimately, the combined effect of the transformative use doctrine and the idea/expression dichotomy is to affirm that AI can play a lawful, ethical, and creative role in the pursuit of knowledge —

particularly when that role is framed as collaborative rather than substitutive. Educators and theological institutions should not fear AI, nor should they delegate their intellectual authority to it. Instead, they should use it as a tool that supports curiosity, enhances precision, and opens up new possibilities for inquiry and communication.

As laws evolve, and as court decisions begin to clarify the boundaries of fair use and ownership, it will be important for scholars to remain engaged with both legal developments and ethical reflection. AI is not simply a legal problem; it is a pedagogical and moral challenge. How we use it reflects what we value about learning, authorship, and truth.

For theological education in particular, where the transmission and transformation of tradition is central, the question is not merely what AI can do, but how it can be used in a way that honors the vocation of the teacher, the dignity of the learner, and the integrity of the theological enterprise.

Chapter 9
Academic Integrity and Student Cheating

Integrity lies at the heart of all meaningful education. Without it, trust erodes between students and teachers, institutions and communities, and ultimately between learners and the truths they seek. In spiritually-formed educational settings, the call to integrity is not only academic but moral. It reflects a vision of education in which truth is pursued not as mere information, but as something to be lived. The presence of artificial intelligence in academic life challenges this vision in new and urgent ways. As AI tools become increasingly capable of producing essays, analyzing texts, and answering questions with remarkable fluency, the boundaries between authentic learning and artificial assistance have become more difficult to discern.

This chapter addresses the question of academic integrity in the age of AI. It considers how institutions and educators might respond to the growing potential for student misuse of AI tools, not only by enforcing rules but by cultivating ethical awareness and communal responsibility. The challenge is not merely to prevent cheating, but to foster environments in which honesty, intellectual humility, and the pursuit of wisdom are seen as integral to one's spiritual and scholarly development.

In any generation, students have faced temptations to take shortcuts in their academic work. These temptations are not new, but the tools now available make it far easier to fabricate competence. A student struggling to complete an essay on divine mercy in the prophetic literature can, in seconds, ask a language model to generate a coherent argument replete with scriptural citations. Another student, unsure how to frame a response to a difficult theological reading, may prompt an AI to summarize and evaluate the text, then pass the response off as their own. Such uses are increasingly difficult to detect, especially when students are strategic in editing the output or using paraphrasing tools to obscure its origins.

The deeper concern, however, is not merely detection. It is deformation. When students habitually outsource their thinking, they weaken the very muscles that spiritual and academic formation depend upon: patience, attentiveness, interpretation, and discernment. The practices that develop insight and character — struggling with a difficult passage, articulating a question imperfectly, learning from failure — are bypassed in favor of polished but hollow performance. Over time, this undermines not only the quality of education but the integrity of the person.

Many institutions are now seeking to respond through policy, updating academic honesty guidelines to address AI tools directly. Some prohibit the use of generative AI unless explicitly permitted. Others require students to cite AI assistance in the same way they would cite other sources. Still others are experimenting with new categories of collaboration and support, recognizing that AI may, in some cases, be a legitimate aid to learning when used transparently.

Policies alone, however, are insufficient. They must be grounded in a culture of integrity — a shared understanding that honesty is not simply about avoiding punishment but about honoring the educational process itself. In spiritually-rooted institutions, this culture should be shaped by traditions of moral formation, communal accountability, and vocational reflection. The Hebrew prophets condemned deceit not only as a violation of the law but as a rupture of covenant. The Gospels place truth at the center of discipleship, even when it comes at personal cost. Early monastic traditions emphasized integrity in thought and word as signs of an undivided heart. These sources do not offer administrative policies, but they provide a moral horizon within which policies might take shape.

Faculty play a key role in shaping this culture. They can model integrity by discussing their own practices of study and inquiry — how they use AI tools, how they cite their sources, and how they make space for reflection in their intellectual life. They can frame assignments not only as tasks to be completed but as opportunities for students to encounter something of significance. A professor assigning a paper on the nature of hope in Paul's letters might begin by asking students how they have encountered hope in their own lives, inviting them to see the connection between exegesis and existential reflection. In this way, the assignment becomes not just an academic hurdle but a formative exercise.

Conversations about integrity should also be embedded into the rhythm of the course. Rather than issuing a warning on the first day and revisiting it only when a problem arises, instructors can return regularly to questions of authorship, voice, and responsibility. When discussing Augustine's *Confessions*, for example, one might explore not only his theological insights but his literary honesty — the way he names his struggles, confesses his failures, and seeks truth with vulnerability. When teaching the Psalms, one might reflect with students on how lament and praise require authenticity, and how the same authenticity is required in academic and spiritual expression alike.

Assignments can also be designed to support integrity. Prompts that require personal reflection, contextual application, or dialogical engagement are more resistant to misuse. Instead of asking for a general essay on the image of God, an instructor might ask students to compare that doctrine to their experience of community life, their understanding of justice, or their engagement with current events. Group work, oral presentations, and creative projects can provide additional avenues for demonstrating learning in ways that are difficult to fake and easier to affirm.

At the institutional level, academic integrity offices, student life departments, and chaplaincies can collaborate to address the broader moral questions AI raises. Workshops on ethical research, faculty panels on technology and formation, or retreats on vocation in a digital age can all contribute to a shared understanding that integrity is not an individual burden but a communal task. The goal is not to surveil but to shepherd, not to punish but to form.

It is also important to recognize that the temptation to misuse AI is often a symptom of deeper struggles — time pressure, academic anxiety, imposter syndrome, or spiritual fatigue. In this light, punitive responses to academic dishonesty may not be sufficient. Institutions must attend to the conditions under which students are making these decisions and offer support accordingly. Advising structures, mental health resources, mentoring relationships, and spiritual care all contribute to an environment where students feel empowered to do their own work — and to grow in the process.

In the age of AI, academic integrity cannot be maintained by suspicion or software alone. It must be nourished by trust, by meaningful relationships, and by a shared commitment to truth. Educators and institutions have the opportunity not only to respond to the challenges of cheating but to reclaim a richer vision of education—one in which learning is understood as a journey of formation, and where the tools we use are always subordinate to the kind of persons we are becoming.

As we turn to the next chapter, we move from individual practices to institutional strategy. The question now becomes: How can schools prepare themselves structurally, pedagogically, and spiritually for a future in which AI will be a constant presence? What kind of policies, resources, and training will be needed to equip faculty and students for wise and faithful engagement?

Chapter 10
Theological and Ethical Reflections on AI

The advent of artificial intelligence in education, research, and daily life compels more than pragmatic adjustment. It demands theological and ethical reflection. What does it mean to create machines that mimic human intelligence, produce speech that sounds like wisdom, or imitate forms of presence once reserved for persons? What are the limits of such imitation? And what does the use of AI reveal about our own desires, fears, and visions of what it means to be human?

In spiritually-informed traditions, questions of technology are never only about utility. They are also about anthropology, ethics, and the moral shape of community. Technology is not neutral; it reflects the values of its creators, the practices of its users, and the structures of power within which it is embedded. This chapter seeks to bring theological resources to bear on the ethical evaluation of artificial intelligence, not by offering a final verdict, but by identifying frameworks for ongoing discernment.

At the center of any theological account of AI must be the question of the human person. If AI systems can generate text, compose music, translate languages, and engage in conversation, what distinguishes human intelligence from artificial replication? The answer lies not in speed or sophistication but in relational and spiritual depth. Human beings are not simply processors of data. They are creatures formed in relationship—capable of love, self-reflection, vulnerability, and communion. In the biblical vision, humans are not defined solely by their mental capacity but by their vocation to steward creation, seek wisdom, and live in covenant with others and with God.

This vision resists both romanticism and reduction. It does not require that humans be infallible or omniscient, but it insists that they are more than the sum of their outputs. Intelligence, in this light, is not merely a function of correct answers or efficient processing. It is shaped by moral memory, spiritual longing, and the capacity for transformation. These are *qualities AI does not possess. Language models may be trained on sacred texts, but they do not believe, worship, lament, or rejoice. They cannot pray. They cannot discern the movement of the Spirit or respond to suffering with compassion rooted in history and hope. Their eloquence is impressive, but it is empty of presence.*

This distinction has ethical implications. One danger in the use of AI is not only that it might deceive others, but that it might deceive us — leading us to treat machines as if they were agents, or to forget the spiritual and relational dimensions of human action. When AI is used to write pastoral letters, generate prayers, or simulate ethical debate, we risk confusing linguistic performance with moral responsibility. A well-phrased blessing generated by a machine may sound moving, but it is not born of love. A sermon outline may be structurally sound, but it carries no spiritual authority. It has not emerged from fasting, intercession, or the shared life of a community.

Moreover, AI is not only a mirror of human thought but a product of human culture — shaped by the assumptions, exclusions, and biases of the data on which it is trained. Language models reproduce dominant narratives, marginalize minority voices, and reflect the inequalities of the societies that produce them. For educators committed to justice, equity, and reconciliation, this presents a serious challenge. One must ask: Whose perspectives are being amplified? Whose stories are being ignored? How do we resist the flattening of moral complexity into algorithmic convenience?

Here, theological ethics can offer guidance. The prophetic tradition, for example, calls attention to the ways in which power distorts perception and speech. The prophets do not merely proclaim truth; they uncover falsehoods masked in pious language. They call out systems that appear righteous but are built on exploitation. In this spirit, educators and scholars must ask whether AI systems—however impressive—serve or undermine the dignity of the poor, the marginalized, and the voiceless. Do these tools challenge injustice, or do they reinforce existing hierarchies of knowledge, language, and access?

The ethics of AI also intersects with questions of formation. If these tools shape how we learn, what kind of learners do they produce? Are students being formed in habits of inquiry, patience, and dialogue—or in habits of efficiency, mimicry, and disengagement? Are faculty being encouraged to mentor, model, and accompany—or to delegate formation to machines? These are not technological questions alone. They are questions about what kind of persons and communities we are seeking to cultivate.

Another relevant concern is the temptation toward technological messianism—the belief that AI can solve human problems once and for all. This temptation is not new. Throughout history, humans have turned to idols of their own making in search of certainty, control, and deliverance. Whether in golden calves or silver screens, the longing for power without vulnerability remains potent. In the digital age, AI can become one more such idol: a source of knowledge without accountability, presence without relationship, or power without wisdom.

A theological vision resists this temptation by affirming finitude as a gift. Human limitations are not flaws to be overcome but conditions for humility, dependence, and community. Technology, rightly ordered, may extend human capacity. But when it seeks to replace vulnerability with invincibility, or embodiment with simulation, it distorts the very fabric of moral and spiritual life. Wisdom begins not with mastery but with reverence — with the recognition that knowledge must be guided by love, and that truth must be embodied in lives of justice and peace.

This does not mean that AI should be rejected wholesale. On the contrary, tools of great power require careful stewardship. In the parables, servants are praised not for burying their talents, but for investing them with discernment and courage. The same applies to technological gifts. The task is to use them in ways that align with deeper commitments — to form students, serve communities, support learning, and deepen the life of the spirit. AI may assist in these aims, but it cannot define them.

In discerning how to use AI, educators and institutions must therefore return to fundamental questions: What do we believe about human dignity, purpose, and destiny? What kind of knowledge leads to wisdom? What kind of teaching fosters transformation? And what kind of world are we preparing students to inhabit, shape, and serve?

Theological and ethical reflection on AI is still in its early stages, and it will require voices from many traditions, disciplines, and cultures. But it must begin now, not only in theory but in practice — in classrooms, policies, assignments, and conversations. For those who see education as a sacred trust, the emergence of AI is not a distraction. It is an invitation: to ask again what it means to teach, to learn, and to seek truth in a world where machines speak—but only humans are called to love.

In the next chapter, we will explore how institutions can respond at a structural level: developing strategy, training faculty, crafting policy, and cultivating leadership capable of guiding communities through the promises and perils of artificial intelligence.

Chapter 11
Institutional Strategy and Faculty Development

The emergence of artificial intelligence in higher education is not a passing trend. It represents a structural transformation that will shape pedagogy, research, assessment, and administration for years to come. While individual faculty members and students are already making decisions about how to use or resist these tools, the long-term impact of AI will depend, in large part, on how institutions respond—how they organize, educate, support, and govern themselves in a time of rapid technological change.

For institutions grounded in spiritual and moral traditions, this response must be more than tactical. It must be theological, ethical, and formational. How can schools prepare their faculty and communities to use AI wisely? How can they craft policies that are both clear and compassionate, visionary and realistic? What does it mean for a school to steward new technologies in light of its mission—not only to educate minds but to form hearts, cultivate virtues, and serve the common good?

This chapter explores the strategic and developmental dimensions of institutional engagement with AI. It focuses on three core areas: faculty development, policy and governance, and institutional culture. Together, these dimensions form the foundation for long-term fidelity and flexibility in a world increasingly shaped by intelligent machines.

Faculty are at the heart of any educational institution. Their decisions—what to assign, how to teach, when to allow or prohibit AI use — will shape the student experience far more than any policy document. *Yet many faculty, even those deeply experienced in pedagogy or scholarship, feel unprepared for the ethical and practical questions AI introduces.* They may be unsure how the technology works, wary of its biases, or unclear about how to talk to students about it. Others may be eager to experiment but uncertain how to do so without compromising integrity or depth.

In this context, faculty development becomes essential. Institutions must provide opportunities for educators to learn about AI in ways that are both technically accurate and spiritually grounded. Workshops, reading groups, and faculty learning communities can offer spaces to explore how AI tools function, what their pedagogical uses might be, and where their dangers lie. Such programs should include not only demonstrations of emerging tools, but also theological and ethical reflection on what these tools mean for the vocation of teaching.

Faculty should be equipped not only with information, but with frameworks for discernment. They should be encouraged to ask: Does this technology support the kind of learning I want to cultivate? Does it foster student growth in wisdom, integrity, and compassion? Does it align with the mission of the institution and the spirit of the tradition in which we teach? Training that integrates technical literacy with moral reflection will be far more fruitful than approaches that treat AI as merely a new gadget or administrative challenge.

Policy is another critical area of institutional strategy. Schools must craft clear, accessible guidelines on the appropriate use of AI in academic work. These policies should articulate when and how students may use AI tools, how such use should be cited or acknowledged, and what constitutes misuse or dishonesty. Policies should also recognize the complexity of AI usage—for example, distinguishing between using AI for basic grammar correction versus using it to generate entire essays. Blanket prohibitions may be easy to write but hard to enforce, and they may prevent thoughtful engagement with tools that, when used appropriately, could enhance learning.

Good policy also includes proactive guidance. Institutions can develop resource pages, model assignment language, and suggested syllabus statements that clarify expectations without fear or ambiguity. Faculty should not have to invent these resources from scratch. Nor should they be expected to monitor AI use in isolation. *A coordinated institutional response—across academic affairs, student life, libraries, and IT—is essential.*

Moreover, policy must be framed not only in legal or punitive terms, but in terms that reflect institutional mission. A policy grounded in a vision of formation, hospitality, truthfulness, and shared responsibility will resonate more deeply than one framed solely in terms of compliance. Such language draws on the same sources that inspire teaching and worship: the call to live honestly, the imperative to love neighbor through integrity, and the belief that learning is a sacred trust.

Beyond faculty training and formal policy, institutions must attend to the broader culture in which technology is discussed, deployed, and discerned. Is the conversation about AI taking place only in tech committees or IT offices, or is it part of faculty meetings, chapel discussions, and strategic planning? Are students being invited to reflect on how AI shapes their habits of learning, their self-understanding, their prayer life, or their moral imagination? Are staff and administrators being supported in thinking about how these tools affect advising, mentoring, and student services?

A spiritually-informed institutional culture will not treat AI as a neutral tool. Nor will it respond with panic or passivity. It will instead approach this moment as an opportunity for collective discernment. Schools might hold community forums on technology and vocation, bring in guest speakers to challenge assumptions, or invite faculty and students to share stories of both success and struggle in using AI. Such conversations cultivate a climate in which questions are welcome and wisdom is shared.

In this kind of culture, *experimentation is encouraged, but accountability is preserved.* Faculty might be invited to pilot AI-integrated assignments, with structured reflection and student feedback. Assessment offices might explore how AI affects outcomes and engagement. Chaplaincies or spiritual life offices might host theological discussions on machine learning, human personhood, and digital justice. The goal is not uniformity but coherence: a diverse but shared commitment to using technology in ways that support the flourishing of students and communities.

Leadership plays a decisive role in shaping this institutional posture. Presidents, provosts, deans, and department chairs must not only authorize policy but embody vision. They must be willing to speak publicly about the ethical challenges AI presents, to invest in professional development, and to model the kind of humility and curiosity that characterizes a learning community. They must also recognize that AI will not affect only teaching and learning, but also fundraising, admissions, strategic communications, and long-term planning. Leadership must be both comprehensive and grounded.

Finally, institutions must think long-term. AI is not a single technology but an evolving field. New models will emerge, regulatory landscapes will shift, and student expectations will change. Schools should establish processes for ongoing review, interdisciplinary task forces for innovation and ethics, and partnerships with other institutions facing similar questions. They should invest in research, support public scholarship on AI and theology, and build institutional memory that can guide future generations.

The spiritual traditions that undergird many of these institutions offer resources for such sustained reflection. They remind us that wisdom takes time, that discernment is a communal task, and that our tools must always serve our deepest values — not the other way around. *The future of theological education in an AI age will not be shaped only by what we know, but by how we choose to act — with integrity, imagination, and hope.*

The next chapter turns toward that future more directly. What might it mean to reimagine spiritually-rooted education in light of these emerging technologies? How might AI invite — not merely threaten — new forms of formation, collaboration, and global connection?

Chapter 12
Reimagining Education with AI

Artificial intelligence has often been framed as a threat to education — as a force that will replace teachers, erode integrity, and flatten learning into mechanical efficiency. These concerns are not without merit. Yet they are only part of the story. *The deeper challenge — and opportunity — is not merely to manage AI but to imagine with it.* For institutions shaped by traditions of wisdom, spiritual formation, and moral inquiry, the task is not to conform to technological change but to lead within it. *This requires vision: not reactive control, but creative discernment.*

This chapter considers how artificial intelligence might invite a reimagining of education itself — its practices, structures, purposes, and global reach. It does not deny the risks AI poses. Rather, it asks what becomes possible when the tools of automation and augmentation are placed in the service of transformation. What if AI were not a substitute for education, but a companion to its deepest aims?

One place to begin is pedagogy. Traditional models of education have often relied on fixed schedules, uniform delivery, and standardized assessment. These structures have served institutions well, but they have also left many learners behind — those with different learning styles, linguistic backgrounds, or work and family obligations. AI tools now offer the possibility of personalized, adaptive learning environments in which students receive support tailored to their pace, context, and prior knowledge. A student struggling with theological terminology might receive simplified definitions, scaffolded readings, or real-time explanations. Another student with deep background in a subject might be offered advanced commentary, parallel traditions, or integrative challenges.

Such adaptability can be especially powerful in global or multilingual classrooms. AI-based translation, summarization, and multimedia tools can make lectures, readings, and discussions accessible across linguistic boundaries. A seminary student in Nairobi might study alongside a peer in São Paulo, both reading a mystic from the fourth century and a poet from the twenty-first, aided by AI tools that bridge their languages and connect their contexts. In this way, education becomes not only more inclusive, but more interwoven — reflecting the diversity and unity of the body it seeks to serve.

Curricular design may also be reimagined. With AI's capacity to organize and visualize large bodies of knowledge, educators can create dynamic maps of theological, historical, and ethical content. These maps can show how doctrines develop, how biblical themes recur across cultures, how spiritual practices emerge and adapt over time. Students can explore these networks interactively, tracing their own paths, asking their own questions, and contributing their own insights. Such an approach moves beyond passive reception toward active construction of meaning.

Instructors, rather than serving primarily as dispensers of content, become curators of learning environments, mentors of discernment, and facilitators of dialogue. They guide students not only through subjects, but toward wisdom. AI, in this model, becomes a tool not of control but of possibility — freeing time, expanding access, and enriching engagement.

AI also enables new modes of collaborative learning. Students can co-create annotated commentaries, share devotional reflections linked to biblical texts, or build collective archives of justice movements and theological responses. These shared projects can span institutions, languages, and disciplines, forming networks of inquiry that mirror the early epistolary communities — linked not by geography alone, but by shared devotion to truth and love.

In research, AI may support the discovery of voices too often overlooked — texts untranslated, traditions underrepresented, patterns unrecognized by conventional methods. Scholars can use AI to surface neglected sermons, compare spiritual metaphors across centuries, or trace ethical themes in disparate cultural settings. When paired with ethical review and theological reflection, such tools may not only advance scholarship but democratize it.

Even formation itself may be enhanced — not replaced — by careful use of AI. Guided journaling prompts, personalized spiritual exercises, and multilingual access to ancient prayers and practices can support students in integrating their learning with their interior life. AI cannot form the soul. But it may help students attend to the soul's questions more deeply, if used wisely.

Institutionally, AI invites rethinking not only pedagogy but mission. Schools can expand their reach beyond conventional degree programs, offering modular learning, community-based education, and spiritual resources to underserved populations. They can partner with churches, NGOs, and global movements to share knowledge, build capacity, and learn together. In an era of growing inequality and ecological urgency, AI may allow institutions to become more nimble, more responsive, and more prophetic —

less constrained by legacy systems, more open to collaboration and innovation.

Yet this reimagining must remain grounded. AI should not become a new form of empire, replicating structures of dominance through digital means. It must be guided by commitments to justice, truth, and solidarity. It must be shaped by the voices of those on the margins, and accountable to communities it seeks to serve. For this reason, the task of reimagining education is not primarily technical. It is spiritual.

Educators, administrators, students, and communities must come together to ask: What kind of formation is needed for our time? What kind of knowledge heals? What kind of community reflects the character of the One who calls us to teach, to learn, and to live in love? These are not questions AI can answer. But they are questions AI can help us pursue, if we bring to its use the same attentiveness we bring to the classroom, the text, and the face of our neighbor.

This vision does not require abandoning tradition. On the contrary, it draws from the same sources that have always animated theological education: the sacred texts, the wisdom of the elders, the witness of the saints, the yearning of the heart. It asks only that we remain open — that we do not fear change more than we fear irrelevance, and that we do not worship novelty more than we love the good.

Artificial intelligence is not the future of education. But it will be part of it. The future remains human, relational, and spiritually alive. It remains, in the deepest sense, a mystery — one not to be controlled, but to be entered with reverence, hope, and courage.

The next chapter will turn to those who are already walking this path: educators and institutions experimenting with AI in thoughtful, grounded, and creative ways. Their stories offer not only caution but inspiration, showing what is possible when wisdom and imagination work together in the service of learning.

Chapter 13
Case Studies and Voices from the Field

The preceding chapters have offered theological reflection, pedagogical frameworks, and institutional guidance for engaging artificial intelligence in spiritually-formed education. Yet theory must be tested by practice. Across schools, seminaries, and learning communities, educators are already experimenting with AI—not as a replacement for formation, but as a partner in it. They are innovating, stumbling, learning, and imagining what might be possible when wisdom leads technology.

This chapter offers a selection of case studies and vignettes from educators and institutions exploring the use of AI in spiritually-rooted settings. These examples are not intended as models to be replicated uncritically. Rather, they serve as conversation starters, windows into practice, and testimonies to the creativity and care that animate this work.

Teaching with AI-Assisted Dialogue: A Classroom in the Psalms

At a small theological college in the Midwest, a professor of Hebrew poetry redesigned her "Psalms and the Life of Prayer" course to incorporate AI-based dialogue partners. Students were assigned specific psalms—laments, praises, wisdom texts—and tasked with crafting reflection pieces from the voice of an ancient worshiper. To support historical imagination, students used an AI tool trained on biblical texts and commentaries to simulate dialogue between the assigned psalm and a contemporary voice of protest, grief, or praise.

The professor reported that while the AI sometimes flattened nuance, it also prompted students to ask better questions. They debated whether machines could "pray," reflected on the difference between reciting and believing, and explored how lament functions differently when issued by a machine versus a person who has suffered. The goal was never to let the AI interpret the text on behalf of the student, but to serve as a reflective foil. The result was not only improved exegetical skills but deeper engagement with the spiritual and emotional dimensions of the Psalms.

Redesigning Assessment in a Homiletics Program

At a seminary in East Africa, faculty were concerned about increasing reliance on AI-generated sermons. Instructors found that students were submitting homiletic outlines that mirrored AI model outputs—with clean structure but little depth, local resonance, or lived theology.

Rather than respond punitively, the faculty decided to restructure the final project. Students were now required to preach their sermons in community settings (churches, refugee centers, or agricultural collectives), then submit a reflective paper that documented the process: contextual research, biblical and theological grounding, listener responses, and personal growth.

AI was allowed—but only as an acknowledged tool during brainstorming. Students who used AI to sketch ideas were expected to explain how they revised or rejected its suggestions. The resulting sermons were more grounded, less formulaic, and far more transformative. Instructors noted a return to spiritual preparation, relational listening, and contextual discernment—what one faculty member described as "real preaching again."

AI in Research: Amplifying Underrepresented Voices

A faculty member at a theological institute in Brazil used AI to conduct textual analysis across hundreds of liberation theology essays, many previously unavailable in English. The project's aim was to trace the emergence of ecological themes in theological reflection from 1970 to the present.

AI-assisted translation and clustering tools enabled the researcher to identify patterns, surface lesser-known voices, and publish a multilingual annotated bibliography. While the scholar reviewed all translations manually and rejected machine interpretations that distorted the original tone, they reported that AI allowed them to access far more material than would have been possible alone.

The project did not eliminate the researcher's role—it expanded it. AI served as a lantern, not a guide. Its value lay not in replacing interpretation, but in making room for more faithful engagement with the breadth of the tradition.

Faculty Formation: Building a Learning Cohort

At a theological school in Southeast Asia, an academic dean launched a year-long AI faculty learning cohort. The program gathered faculty from biblical studies, pastoral theology, ethics, and liturgics to learn how AI tools might enhance—or hinder—their work.

The cohort met monthly, exploring a shared reading list, testing educational tools, and reflecting on theological implications. Some sessions featured demonstrations of AI in curriculum design; others invited reflection on personhood, embodiment, and community in the digital age. Faculty were encouraged to experiment in small ways: an AI-generated glossary here, an interactive dialogue there.

By the end of the year, each faculty member submitted a "personal AI teaching statement" and a revised syllabus incorporating their learning. More than the tools themselves, participants valued the space for dialogue, fear-sharing, and ethical reflection. As one professor remarked, "The real gift was permission to not know — and to imagine together."

Digital Spiritual Practices and Global Formation

An ecumenical formation program serving dispersed students across the African diaspora introduced a digital spiritual practices module supported by AI. Students could engage in guided prayer, receive contextualized Scripture reflections in their first languages, and build a personal liturgical calendar that drew on multiple traditions.

AI tools assisted in adapting devotional resources to the student's schedule, focus, or prayer style, offering brief morning readings, historical insights, or prompts for journaling. While all content was vetted by faculty, students had significant agency in shaping their devotional rhythm. The feedback from students was overwhelmingly positive. They described feeling more connected to the wider church, more grounded in daily practice, and more supported in times of stress.

Faculty remained clear that AI could not form character — but it could support attentiveness. As one formation director noted, *"The Spirit moves in the silence. But sometimes AI helps us remember to make room for it."*

These case studies do not offer a single conclusion. Some point to the power of AI to expand access, others to its ability to provoke ethical questions or encourage pedagogical redesign. Together, they suggest that engagement with AI need not be defensive or superficial. When approached with humility, courage, and creativity, these tools may become allies in the long work of education and formation.

To do so, however, requires institutions and educators to remain clear about their purpose. AI is not an answer. It is an accelerant. It amplifies what is already present—in our pedagogy, our values, our hopes, and our fears. If we want our students to become wise, truthful, and compassionate, we must cultivate those same qualities in ourselves and in the systems we build.

Part IV
Prompt Engineering
What Makes AI Work Well

Chapter 14
Prompting with Purpose
Foundations for Theological AI Use

Artificial intelligence is transforming the way we think, write, research, and teach. While many in theological education are rightly cautious about these shifts, others are beginning to recognize that AI, when used with wisdom and integrity, can become a valuable companion in the pursuit of truth. Among the most significant skills emerging in this landscape is prompt engineering—the ability to communicate effectively with AI tools through well-crafted questions and instructions.

Prompt engineering is not merely technical. It is a form of theological inquiry. To prompt well is to ask good questions. And to ask good questions is to pursue clarity, curiosity, and discernment—virtues long cultivated in theological traditions. Just as theological reflection is shaped by how one frames a question—whether doctrinal, biblical, pastoral, or ethical—so too does the quality of an AI-generated response depend on how the prompt is constructed.

This chapter is written for educators, researchers, students, and leaders in theological institutions who wish to engage AI tools faithfully and practically. It offers not a theoretical overview of artificial intelligence, but a hands-on guide to crafting better prompts for the work of theological study, teaching, writing, and formation.

Why Prompt Engineering Matters in Theological Work

Artificial intelligence can assist theological education most profoundly at two pivotal moments: at the beginning of a project, and at its end.

At the beginning, AI can help stimulate curiosity, map a field of inquiry, surface hidden connections, and organize initial ideas. With a few well-crafted prompts, one can generate a range of questions, compare positions across traditions, or visualize how a doctrine like incarnation intersects with themes such as embodiment, suffering, and justice.

At the end of a project, AI can serve as a reviewer and refiner. It can highlight gaps in argumentation, suggest improvements to transitions, help clarify theological phrasing, and even check for tone consistency — offering a mirror that helps the writer polish what has already been carefully composed.

In both cases, the user remains responsible. AI cannot decide what matters. It cannot pray, interpret scripture through the lens of faith, or understand the spiritual significance of a theological argument. But it can serve as a responsive, flexible, and immensely capable tool for those who are committed to theological depth and educational excellence.

The Anatomy of a Good Prompt

Prompt engineering depends on clarity of instruction, context, and purpose. A well-constructed prompt usually contains four key elements:

Instruction – What is the task?

Context – What is the topic, subject, or genre?

Constraints – What limitations or specifications should guide the output?

Perspective or Role – From what voice, background, or disciplinary lens should the AI respond?

The more thoughtfully a prompt is crafted, the more useful the response becomes. Below are specific examples demonstrating these principles in action, tailored to common tasks in theological education.

Example 1: Biblical Interpretation – Broad Prompt vs. Specific Prompt

Basic Prompt:

"Explain the Book of Revelation."

Improved Prompt:

"As a biblical scholar writing for a seminary audience, summarize the main theological themes of the Book of Revelation in 300 words, with particular attention to apocalyptic imagery and pastoral encouragement."

Explanation:

The improved prompt includes a role (biblical scholar), a clear audience (seminary), a task (summarize), a constraint (300 words), and a focus (themes, imagery, encouragement). This specificity helps avoid generic or sensationalistic output.

Example 2: Doctrinal Comparison – Prompting for Analysis

Basic Prompt:

"Compare atonement theories."

Improved Prompt:

"Compare penal substitution and moral influence theories of atonement in 500 words. Present each view fairly and include one historical theologian associated with each."

Explanation:

By requesting fairness, a word count, and historical examples, the prompt steers the AI toward structured, comparative content suitable for academic use.

Example 3: Ethical Application – Contextual Prompting

Basic Prompt:

"What does the Bible say about justice?"

Improved Prompt:

"From the perspective of Old Testament prophetic literature, outline how the concept of justice is framed in Amos and Micah. Limit your summary to 250 words and emphasize implications for economic ethics today."

Explanation:

This prompt gives clear thematic focus (prophets), scope (Amos and Micah), and application (economic ethics), making the response far more usable in classroom or sermon preparation.

Example 4: Patristic Theology – Prompting for Historical Synthesis

Basic Prompt:

"Who is Augustine?"

Improved Prompt:

"Summarize Augustine's view of grace and free will as presented in his writings against Pelagius. Use a tone suitable for graduate theological students and keep the explanation under 400 words."

Explanation:

The task is historically located, the theme (grace and free will) is specified, and the audience and tone are defined.

Example 5: Stylistic and Devotional Adaptation

Prompt for stylistic tone adjustment:

"Rewrite this paragraph to make it more meditative and suitable for a devotional reflection, while keeping the theological ideas intact."

Prompt for audience shift:
"Simplify this explanation of perichoresis for use in a lay adult education class."
Explanation:
These prompts ask AI to adjust not content, but style, tone, and accessibility — crucial for teaching and formation across contexts.

Example 6: Iterative Refinement
Often, the best responses come through a series of prompts rather than one. For example:
Step 1: "Outline five key theological themes in the Gospel of Luke."
Step 2: "Expand the third theme into a full paragraph with scriptural references."
Step 3: "Summarize that paragraph in one sentence for use in a sermon introduction."
This iterative strategy reflects the actual flow of academic writing and formation — explore, deepen, distill.

Prompt engineering is not about finding the one perfect prompt. It is about cultivating habits of questioning, refining, and rethinking. These are theological habits as well. When we craft better prompts, we learn not only how to use a machine more effectively — we learn how to think more clearly, write more honestly, and teach more attentively.
The chapters that follow will build on this foundation by walking step-by-step through the core activities of theological education and research — writing, editing, teaching, and formation — each with its own prompting strategies, examples, and best practices.

Chapter 15
Prompting for Research and Theological Writing

Prompt engineering can be one of the most powerful tools at your disposal in theological research. Used well, it helps generate questions, compare viewpoints, engage texts, and outline arguments with clarity and theological depth.

Whether you're at the brainstorming stage or refining your thesis structure, the key is how you ask. This chapter gives you ready-to-use prompting strategies for real theological work.

Prompting to Generate Research Questions

When you're just starting out, good prompts can help you move from vague interests to focused theological questions.

Try prompts like:

"List 5 theological questions related to the theme of hope in Romans."

"Generate 3 research questions on the doctrine of creation in African theological contexts."

"What are some underexplored theological issues in Luke–Acts?"

Best practices:

Include your tradition or context (e.g., "liberation theology," "patristic sources")

Limit scope: focus on specific texts or doctrines

Ask for a range of perspectives

Prompting to Compare Theological Views

Comparing theological positions is a key component of academic writing. Use prompts that force the AI to structure comparison thoughtfully.

Examples:

"Compare Augustine's and Pelagius's views of grace and free will. Include scriptural references."

"How do Martin Luther and John Wesley differ in their understanding of sanctification?"

"Create a chart comparing three major atonement theories: penal substitution, moral influence, and *Christus Victor*."

Tips:

Ask for fairness: "Present each view objectively"

Include historical, pastoral, or doctrinal dimensions

Consider follow-up prompts like: "Which view is most prevalent in modern homiletics?"

Prompting to Summarize Classic Texts

Dense theological works can be hard to digest. Use prompts to extract the core arguments and then clarify them for your audience.

Examples:

"Summarize the main argument of Anselm's *Cur Deus Homo* in 250 words for a graduate student."

"What is the core teaching of Bonhoeffer's Discipleship on costly grace?"

"Summarize Aquinas's five ways in simple academic language."

Refinements:
"Now explain this summary to a lay adult Bible study group."

"Give 3 pastoral implications of Bonhoeffer's view of discipleship."

Prompting to Simulate Scholarly Dialogue

Use prompts to create contrast and debate. This is great for preparing classroom discussion, essays, or research framing.

Examples:
"Present a debate between Karl Barth and a process theologian on divine immutability."

"Summarize two opposing views on women's ordination, using theological and biblical arguments."

"You are a 20th-century Catholic ethicist. Respond to a critique of natural law from a liberation theologian."

*Advanced strategy: (*Create a prompt chain)
"Summarize Barth's view of revelation."

"Now critique that view from a feminist theological perspective."

"Propose a synthesis that addresses both concerns."

Prompting to Create and Refine Outlines

Outlining is where AI can help bring shape to your scattered ideas. Prompt it to suggest a structure—and then tailor it.

Examples:
"Create a detailed outline for a 3,000-word essay on the Holy Spirit in Luke–Acts."

"Organize a paper comparing sacramental theology in East and West into 5 sections."

"Draft a lecture outline on divine justice in the Minor Prophets."

Make it better with constraints:

"Include introduction and conclusion."

"Suggest 1–2 key sources for each section."

"Add a discussion question for each section."

Prompting to Explore Theologies from Global and Marginalized Perspectives

AI can help surface perspectives that are sometimes underrepresented—if you prompt it carefully.

Examples:

"List 3 major themes in Latin American liberation theology."

"How have African theologians responded to the Book of Job?"

"Summarize Asian feminist interpretations of the Magnificat."

Be cautious:

Cross-check the theologians and sources mentioned

Ask for names, dates, and citations you can follow up on yourself

Never treat AI as a final source—use it as a pointer

Prompting for Interdisciplinary Integration

Theological research often crosses into ethics, philosophy, and science. Prompting can help generate creative links.

Examples:

"How does the concept of imago Dei relate to current debates in AI ethics?"

"What might cognitive science contribute to sacramental theology?"

"List 3 implications of ecological theology for eschatological preaching."

Prompting for Bibliographic Scaffolding (*Use with Caution!*)

AI can suggest sources, but it often "hallucinates" or invents references. Use it to brainstorm, not to cite.

Safe prompts:

"What theologians are commonly associated with political theology?"

"Name some recent thinkers writing on pneumatology in Pentecostal traditions."

"List major books that explore the cross-cultural reception of the Gospel of John."

Follow-up prompts:

"Give a 1–2 sentence description of each theologian's main work on this topic."

Important: Always verify every suggested citation or source independently.

Final Reminders for Prompting Research and Writing

- Prompt clearly and specifically—don't assume the model knows your context
- Use role-based prompts to shape perspective: "You are a Reformed ethicist…"
- Build prompts iteratively—ask, adjust, deepen

- Use AI to stimulate, not substitute, your own theological thought
- Remember: You are the theologian. AI is a tool — not a teacher, not an oracle

Next, we'll turn to the other end of the writing process — how prompt engineering can help you revise, refine, and sharpen theological writing for clarity, tone, and coherence. Prompting isn't just for brainstorming. It's also for polishing your best ideas until they're ready to teach, preach, or publish.

Chapter 16
Prompting for Writing Improvement and Theological Communication

Once the research is drafted, the work isn't finished—it's only just beginning. Revising theological writing involves sharpening logic, improving clarity, adjusting tone, and ensuring that theological ideas are communicated faithfully and effectively. This is where prompt engineering can shine.

AI can't judge truth, but it can help you write more clearly, more precisely, and more convincingly. In this chapter, you'll learn how to use prompts to improve sentence structure, check flow and transitions, revise for tone, and proofread theological content.

Prompting for Clarity and Readability

Good theological writing should be deep, but also clear. Use prompts to simplify complex sentences, clarify ideas, and eliminate jargon—without losing depth.

Try prompts like:
"Rewrite this paragraph to make it clearer without losing theological precision."

"Simplify this explanation of perichoresis for a second-year seminary student."

"Break this long sentence into two shorter ones while preserving the meaning."

Example:
Original:
"The eschatological vision of Isaiah, rooted in prophetic oracles of restoration, anticipates a cosmic reconciliation that resists reduction to apocalyptic dualism."
Prompt:
"Simplify this for a theologically trained but non-specialist reader."
AI Output (sample):
"Isaiah's vision of the end times points to a restored world. It emphasizes healing and wholeness, without falling into a simplistic good-versus-evil narrative."

Prompting to Revise Paragraph Flow and Structure
Even well-formed ideas can feel disconnected if the transitions are weak. Use AI to analyze paragraph order, coherence, and structure.

Examples:
"Does this paragraph flow logically from the one before it? Suggest a transition sentence if needed."
"Reorganize this paragraph to emphasize the argument's main point more clearly."
"Suggest a better way to open this section."

Bonus Tip: Add "Explain your reasoning" to your prompt to learn how the AI made its choice — great for teaching and learning.

Prompting for Tone: Academic, Pastoral, or Devotional
Theology is written for many audiences. Use prompts to adjust the tone while keeping the content intact.

Common tone types:
>
> Academic – clear, formal, referenced
>
> Pastoral – warm, practical, relational
>
> Devotional – meditative, reflective, personal

Prompt examples:

"Rewrite this section in an academic tone for a theology journal."

"Adjust this paragraph to be suitable for a homily on Good Friday."

"Rephrase this in a more contemplative tone appropriate for a devotional guide."

Before and After Example:

Original (academic):

"Soteriological themes in Luke's Gospel reflect a dynamic interplay between personal repentance and social liberation."

Prompt:

"Make this more pastoral in tone for use in a Bible study."

Output (sample):

"In Luke's Gospel, we see how God's saving work changes hearts and heals communities. Forgiveness leads to freedom — both personally and socially."

Prompting to Eliminate Repetition and Tighten Language

Repetition weakens writing. AI can help spot redundancies and tighten phrasing.

Prompts to try:
"Identify repeated ideas or phrases in this paragraph and suggest edits."
"Make this section more concise while keeping the theological meaning."
"Cut this down by 30% without losing nuance."

Sample edit task:
"This paragraph repeats the same idea about grace three times. Suggest a tighter version."

Prompting for Introductions and Conclusions

AI can help brainstorm stronger openings and closings.

Prompts for introductions:
"Suggest an engaging introduction for a theological essay on the Trinity."
"Write a two-sentence hook for a paper on the ethics of nonviolence."

Prompts for conclusions:
"Summarize the argument and state why it matters for practical theology today."
"Suggest a closing paragraph that points to further study in eschatology."

Prompting for Proofreading and Style Checking

AI can scan for grammar, punctuation, and voice consistency — but always double-check.

Try prompts like:
"Proofread this section for grammar and clarity. Keep a formal academic tone."
"Are there any verb tense inconsistencies or unclear sentences?"

"Check this for passive voice and suggest where to use active verbs."

Caution: Avoid "rewrite this entire piece" prompts unless you're revising only for mechanics. Always protect your own theological voice.

Prompting to Simulate Audience Reception
You can use prompts to imagine how a reader might respond. This is especially useful for classroom writing, sermons, or public essays.

Prompts to try:
"How might a first-year seminary student respond to this explanation of divine transcendence?"
"What questions might a lay reader have after reading this paragraph on election?"
"What parts of this sermon might feel confusing or too academic?"

Prompting for Citation and Footnote Reminders
AI may not cite accurately — but it can remind you where citations are needed.

Safe prompts:
"Suggest where footnotes might be added to support these claims."
"What theological works or authors should be cited to support this paragraph's ideas?"
"List three major theologians who have written on this topic so I can follow up."

Remember: Always verify AI-generated names, titles, and quotes.

Final Prompting Tips for Theological Revision

- Use short, specific prompts: one paragraph at a time is best.
- Ask AI to explain its suggestions: "Why did you recommend this change?"
- Maintain control over tone and voice — your theological identity matters.
- Don't erase complexity; use prompts to clarify, not flatten, your argument.
- Practice layering prompts: revise, review, recheck for coherence.

AI can't do your thinking for you — but it can help make your ideas stronger, your writing clearer, and your theological communication more compelling. As you continue to develop your voice as a scholar, preacher, or teacher, let prompt engineering be part of your revision toolkit — not to replace discernment, but to support it.

Next, we'll turn to the classroom and community: how to prompt for teaching, formation, and student engagement in theological education.

Would you like a prompt template set based on this chapter or a companion student handout for writing revision support?

Chapter 17
Prompting for Teaching, Formation, and Theological Classroom Practice

Prompt engineering isn't just for research and writing. It also opens up powerful opportunities in the classroom, the curriculum, and the spiritual formation of students. *When used wisely, AI can help educators create materials, train students in theological reasoning, and model discernment in a rapidly evolving digital world.*

This chapter shows how to:

- Design assignments with AI in mind;
- Use prompts to generate lesson plans, reading aids, and case studies;
- Equip students to write and analyze prompts critically; and
- Cultivate theological reflection and vocational discernment through AI-enhanced tasks.

Prompting to Design Theologically-Rich Assignments

AI can help you quickly generate or refine assignments tailored to different learning levels and goals.

Try prompts like:

"Create a 3-part assignment on the doctrine of creation for an MDiv-level theology course."

"Design a classroom activity exploring the use of lament psalms in pastoral care."

"Suggest 3 essay questions on the concept of the kingdom of God in Mark's Gospel."

Refinements:

Add learning objectives: "Include goals aligned with Bloom's taxonomy."

Add assessment methods: "Suggest a grading rubric for this assignment."

Essay prompt: "Compare and contrast two theological interpretations of *kenosis* in Philippians 2. How might each shape a community's understanding of power and humility?"

Case study: "Write a scenario in which a pastor must respond to a congregant's question about hell, reflecting two major theological approaches."

Prompting to Create Lesson Plans, Lectures, and Guides

Let AI assist with first drafts of course prep—especially outlines, reading prompts, and framing questions.

Prompt examples:

"Generate a 45-minute lecture outline on the development of Trinitarian doctrine in the early church."

"Write a set of 5 discussion questions on the Sermon on the Mount that connect to contemporary ethical issues."

"Create a comparative chart of covenant theology in Genesis, Exodus, and Deuteronomy."

Tips:

Ask for learning outcomes: "What should students understand by the end of this session?"

Prompt AI to scaffold difficulty: "List 3 warm-up questions, then 2 deeper challenges."

Prompting to Build Reading Aids and Study Guides

Help students engage deeply with texts using AI-generated guides that clarify, contextualize, and provoke discussion.

Examples:

"Summarize James Cone's The Cross and the Lynching Tree in 300 words for second-year theology students."

"List key terms from Teresa of Ávila's Interior Castle and define them in simple academic language."

"Create a study guide for Psalm 139 that highlights theological themes and pastoral applications."

Optional follow-ups:

"Now add two reflection questions for each theme."

"Include a short prayer or spiritual exercise connected to this reading."

Prompting to Train Students in Prompt Engineering

Teaching students to craft, refine, and evaluate prompts helps them think more clearly and ethically.

Student learning goals:

Frame better theological questions

Analyze AI outputs critically

Reflect on their own voice and authority as theologians

Assignments that work:

Prompt journals: "Each week, log two prompts you used in research and reflect on their usefulness."

Prompt comparisons: "Give students 2 versions of a prompt. Ask them to compare the quality of responses."

Prompt + critique: "Ask AI for a summary of Luther on justification. Then have students evaluate the summary's theological accuracy."

Sample student prompt practice: "Prompt AI to explain the Nicene Creed in 3 different tones: (1) catechetical, (2) academic, and (3) pastoral."

"Write a prompt asking for 3 interpretations of Romans 9. Then test the results against real commentaries."

Prompting to Model Ethical, Formational Engagement
Educators shape student imagination by showing that AI is a tool to support—not replace—formation.

In teaching, demonstrate how to:
Use AI to explore diverse viewpoints, not flatten complexity

Prompt to deepen questions, not to get "the answer"

Recognize biases, gaps, or generic summaries

Prompt samples to model:
"List 3 ways Augustine's view of evil might speak to trauma theology today. Note any limitations."

"How might a Reformed and a Pentecostal theologian respond differently to Acts 2? Show both voices fairly."

"Offer 2 pastoral reflections on divine hiddenness that reflect different spiritual traditions."

Use in spiritual formation:

"Generate a reflection on *kenosis* (Philippians 2) in the style of a prayer journal entry."

"List 3 spiritual disciplines that correspond to the theology of hospitality in Luke's Gospel."

Reflection prompts for students:

"How did using AI in this assignment affect your own learning, voice, or confidence?"

"What do you think AI understands — and doesn't understand — about faith?"

Prompting for Diverse Classrooms and Intercultural Engagement

For diverse and global classrooms, prompt engineering can help contextualize content and open new dialogues.

Prompts to adapt readings:

"Rewrite this definition of justification for ESL learners in a theological writing course."

"Summarize this article in French and include a glossary of key terms."

"List 3 African or Asian theologians who have written on the Holy Spirit. Briefly summarize their views."

Prompts for comparative theology:

"Compare the doctrine of creation in Orthodox, Indigenous, and Islamic thought. Note areas of overlap and difference."

"Generate questions for interfaith dialogue on human dignity and the image of God."

Final Teaching Prompts to Keep in Mind

- Use prompts to expand—not flatten—your students' theological imagination;
- Invite AI to support personalized learning paths and multilingual access;
- Treat prompt crafting as an exercise in clarity, humility, and curiosity;
- Use class time for critical analysis of AI output—not just AI use; and
- Train students to prompt with conviction and evaluate with care.

AI is now part of the theological classroom. The question is not whether it will be used, but how. Prompt engineering lets us shape its role, invite formation through dialogue, and teach with both innovation and integrity.

With thoughtful use, AI becomes not a threat but a tool for theological educators—expanding access, inviting reflection, and helping the next generation ask sharper questions in the pursuit of wisdom.

Appendix
Sample Institutional AI Policy for
Theological Education

Purpose

This policy outlines the appropriate use of artificial intelligence (AI) tools in academic work and institutional life. It reflects the institution's commitment to academic integrity, spiritual formation, communal trust, and educational excellence in a rapidly evolving technological landscape.

1. Guiding Values

Our institution affirms that:

Technology is a tool to be used in service of wisdom, not a substitute for human insight or spiritual discernment.

Academic work should reflect the authentic engagement, voice, and growth of the student.

Formation is relational, reflective, and embodied; AI must not replace the essential presence of teacher, student, and community.

2. Student Use of AI

a. Permitted Uses

Students may use AI tools (e.g., ChatGPT, Grammarly, translation tools) for brainstorming, grammar correction, summarizing background content, or formatting assistance, unless otherwise restricted by the course instructor.

Students must acknowledge any significant use of AI in the completion of assignments (see Section 5).

b. Prohibited Uses

Submitting AI-generated work as one's own without revision, citation, or instructor permission.

Using AI to complete assessments designed to evaluate original thought, interpretation, or reflection (e.g., essays, sermons, theological reflections) without explicit approval.

Employing AI to circumvent learning objectives or to deceive instructors about the nature of student engagement.

3. Faculty Use of AI

Faculty are encouraged to explore the pedagogical potential of AI tools, including:

- Enhancing accessibility or differentiation in course materials.
- Generating supplemental teaching content.
- Supporting curriculum design or translation.

Faculty should model transparent and ethical use of AI and disclose AI use in syllabus design, assignment creation, or feedback processes when relevant.

4. Institutional Responsibilities

The institution will provide ongoing faculty development opportunities to engage with AI critically and creatively.

Resources, sample syllabus language, and student workshops will be made available to encourage consistent, transparent, and values-aligned engagement with AI.

Academic integrity officers or committees will review this policy annually in light of technological changes and community feedback.

5. Disclosure Guidelines

When students or faculty use AI in the development of academic or instructional content, they must disclose the use with a clear statement, such as:

> Portions of this assignment were generated or assisted by [tool name], including help with [e.g., summarization, outline structure, grammar suggestions]. All content has been reviewed and edited to reflect my own understanding.

Disclosure is required whenever AI contributes substantively to the form or content of the work. Failure to disclose may be treated as a violation of academic integrity.

6. Violations and Accountability

Violations of this policy will be addressed through existing academic honesty procedures, which include opportunities for reflection, repair, and disciplinary action as appropriate. The goal of enforcement is not punishment, but restoration of trust and the upholding of shared commitments.

7. Theological and Ethical Reflection

This institution encourages continued dialogue about the theological, ethical, and pastoral implications of artificial intelligence. We affirm that:

Technology must never replace the work of presence, prayer, or communal discernment.

The human person, made for relationship, cannot be reduced to output or data.

The call to truth remains central to the vocation of teaching and learning.

Glossary of Key Terms

Academic Integrity
The commitment to honesty, trust, and fairness in academic work. In the context of AI, it includes clear guidelines on when and how AI tools may be used or cited.

Algorithm
A set of mathematical rules and procedures that enable a computer to process data, recognize patterns, and make decisions. It forms the foundation of how AI systems learn, adapt, and solve problems across various tasks.

Artificial Intelligence (AI)
The broad field of computer science focused on developing systems that can perform tasks typically requiring human intelligence, such as recognizing speech, interpreting language, generating text, or making decisions based on data.

Data Set
A data set is a structured collection of information used for analysis, training, or reference. In AI, it typically consists of labeled or unlabeled examples — such as text, images, or numbers — organized to help models learn patterns, make predictions, or perform tasks based on real-world or simulated input.

Embedding

A method of converting tokens into numerical vectors, allowing the AI to represent words or concepts in a mathematical space based on contextual relationships.

Generative AI

AI systems capable of creating new content — text, images, music, code — based on learned patterns from training data.

Large Language Model (LLM)

A type of AI system trained on massive quantities of text to predict and generate language. Examples include GPT-4, Claude, and Gemini. These models simulate human-like responses but do not understand content in the human sense.

Machine Learning (ML)

A subset of AI in which systems learn from patterns in data rather than being explicitly programmed. ML underlies most modern AI applications, including language models and recommendation systems.

Prompt

The input or instruction a user gives to an AI model to generate a response. Prompts can be questions, commands, or descriptions.

Prompt Engineering

The practice of crafting effective inputs or questions to guide an AI model's responses. By carefully designing prompts, users can influence output quality, ensuring relevance, clarity, and accuracy in tasks like writing, coding, teaching, or research.

Reinforcement Learning from Human Feedback (RLHF)

A method of refining AI behavior by training it on feedback from human evaluators who rank or rate its responses, aiming to improve helpfulness and reduce harm.

Spiritual Formation

The process of growth in wisdom, character, and faith, often pursued through practices of study, prayer, service, and reflection. In theological education, formation is both personal and communal.

Technological Discernment

The practice of critically evaluating the uses, risks, and spiritual implications of technological tools, especially in educational and pastoral settings.

Tokenization

The process of breaking text into units (tokens) such as words or subword parts that can be processed by language models. Tokens are then mapped to numerical values for computational analysis.

Training

The process of teaching a model to recognize patterns by exposing it to large amounts of data. Through repeated analysis, the model adjusts internal parameters to improve performance on specific tasks, such as language understanding or image recognition.

Transformer Architecture

The neural network design at the core of most advanced LLMs. It uses attention mechanisms to process and generate language, allowing models to consider relationships between all parts of a sentence or passage.

Vector

The numerical representation of data—such as words, images, or sounds—used by AI models to understand relationships and patterns. Vectors allow complex information to be processed mathematically, enabling tasks like similarity comparison, clustering, and semantic reasoning.

www.ingramcontent.com/pod-product-compliance
Lightning Source LLC
La Vergne TN
LVHW021350080426
835508LV00020B/2203